The Mediterranean Pasta Cookbook:

Mediterranean Pasta Recipes for Healthy Living

Nadine Massri

Contents

The Fundamentals

What is the Mediterranean Diet?

The map above shows us the Mediterranean Sea, and the countries that surround it. These countries don't really have much in common, and the same goes for their cuisines; this is actually a good thing. This diet is easy to follow as there will always be a dish to satisfy your craving. Craving something sweet and savoury? A fiery cuisine from morocco is sure to leave you satisfied. Craving something tangy and citrus? Maybe a Greek cuisine is what you're looking for.

Now if the cuisines of these countries are so far apart, why do we categorise their food into one single diet? The answer is simple: It's the healthy ingredients and use of heart-healthy oil. These ingredients are-vegetables, fruits, beans, lentils, whole grains, more seafood than meat and poultry, and heart-healthy olive oil. Different Mediterranean countries cook these ingredients in different ways, but the basics are the same with a focus on health.

The Mediterranean Diet Pyramid

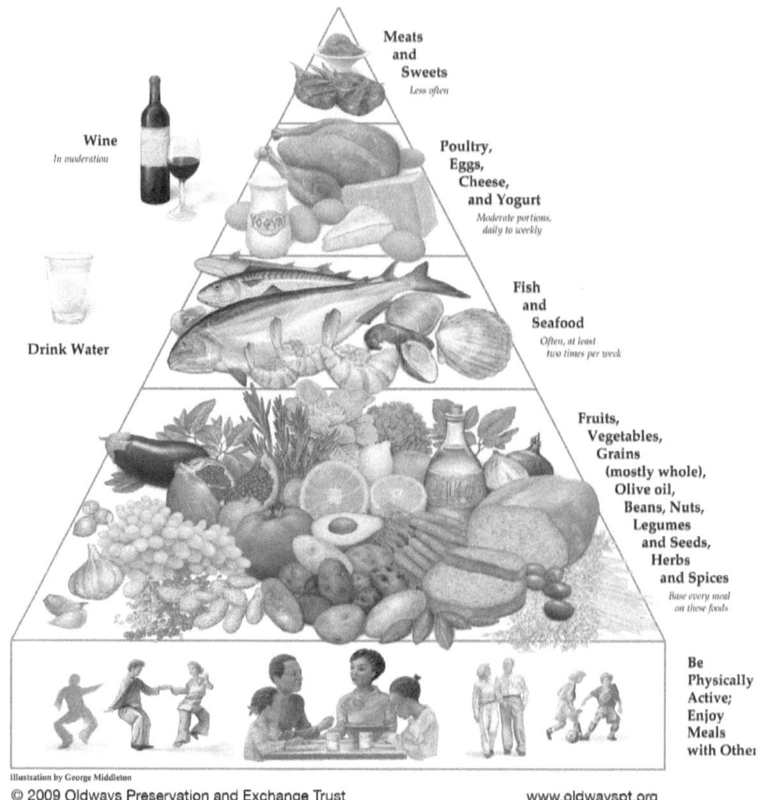

© 2009 Oldways Preservation and Exchange Trust   www.oldwayspt.org

The above graphic illustration from www.oldwatspt.org clearly depicts what the Mediterranean diet, or rather the healthy Mediterranean way of life is based upon. In the year 1950, an American physiologist named Ancel Keys found that the people of Crede had among the lowest rates of coronary heart disease. After thorough research, the physiologist concluded that this was due to their traditional diet, which was loaded with vegetables, grains, and legumes, and included very low saturated fat. Based on this research, the pyramid you see above was formulated in the year 1990. All the recipes in this book have their foundation in the pyramid you see above. Which is to say, that most of the recipes you will find in this book are going to be those of the ingredients you see on the base of the pyramid, and fewer recipes of the ingredients that are placed on the higher levels of the pyramid.

Today, we know that vegetables and olive oil are related to low instances of heart diseases because they are rich in heart-healthy monosaturated fats. Since the Mediterranean diet is loaded with these, it is great for heart health, promotes healthy blood sugar levels, enhances cognitive abilities, and to a certain extent even helps prevent and manage diseases like cancer. The Mediterranean diet isn't low in fat, but today we know that fat doesn't make you fat. Sugar is the culprit. In fact, studies have found that high-fat diets like the popular ketogenic diet can promote fat loss by forcing your body to produce ketones to metabolize the fat, the very same ketones that can also metabolise body fat and hence promote weight loss.

The Mediterranean Flavours

A diet can be the most nutritious diet ever conceived, but it would be pointless if one cannot follow it for more than a day. We are all human, after all, and delicious food is one of the greatest pleasures we get to experience in our ephemeral lifetimes. With that in mind, it is important for any diet to provide the health benefits while tasting absolutely amazing. The Mediterranean diet does exactly that. Since the recipes are from such a wide spectrum of countries, the flavour never gets bland, and with a cookbook like this in your possession, you'll be living the Mediterranean way for years to come!

Although 21 countries have a coastline on the Mediterranean Sea, only a few of these countries truly represent the Mediterranean diet and way of life. Each country has its own flavour, and if you want to get into a little more detail about what the cuisines of a few of the most prominent countries taste like, refer to the table below.

Region	Most Common Ingredients	Overall Cuisine Flavor
Southern Italy	Anchovies, balsamic vinegar, basil, bay leaf, capers, garlic, mozzarella	Italian food is rich and savory, with strongly flavored ingredients. Look for tomato-

		based sauces and even an occasional kick of spicy heat.
	cheese, olive oil, oregano, parsley, peppers, pine nuts, mushrooms, prosciutto, rosemary, sage, thyme, tomatoes	
Greece	Basil, cucumbers, dill, fennel, feta cheese, garlic, honey, lemon, mint, olive oil, oregano, yogurt	Greek cuisines range from tangy with citrus accents to savory. Ingredients like feta cheese add a strong, bold flavor, while yogurt helps provide a creamy texture and soft flavor.
Morocco	Cinnamon, cumin, dried fruits, ginger, lemon, mint, paprika, parsley, pepper, saffron, turmeric	Moroccan cooking uses exotic flavors that include both sweet and savory, often in one dish. The food has strong flavors but isn't necessarily spicy.
Spain	Almonds, anchovies, cheeses (from goats, cows, and sheep), garlic, ham, honey, olive oil, onions, oregano, nuts, paprika, rosemary, saffron, thyme	Garlic and olive oil are a staple when it comes to Spanish dishes. Spanish dishes are often inspired by Arabic and Roman cuisine with emphasis on fresh seafood. Combinations of savory and sweet flavors, such as a seafood stew using sweet paprika are quite common.

Know the Ingredients

Today, we get our ingredients quite differently as compared to how the people living on the Mediterranean coast did 50 years ago. They couldn't just stroll into a grocery store and pick up whatever they wanted. They could only get their hands on what was farmed and fished locally. Today, however, the world is very different and much better connected. You can gain access to ingredients from across the planet with the flick of a finger (if you're shopping for groceries online). Having access to so many options may seem like a hurdle at first, but if you're truly determined to live the Mediterranean way, it has never been easier to do so. All you need to do is include more fresh ingredients into your food, and say no to junk and other processed foods.

Mediterranean Farm Produce

Most of the areas along the Mediterranean Sea are ideal for agriculture due to a moderate climate of wet winters and hot summers. Hence, Mediterranean areas have been growing their own food. Thanks to the climate, olives and fig trees grow well in most of these areas, and naturally have become a staple in the Mediterranean diet.

It is also important to note that relying on fresh produce also means eating seasonally. Not all crops grow all year round, so back in the day there was no option but to eat what was in season. Eating seasonally is highly beneficial as it incorporates a variety of foods into the diet. Today, however, it is easy to eat what you love all-year-round, and this is not a good practice if you do so. Living the Mediterranean way means eating a wide variety of ingredients to get the full spectrum of vitamins and minerals.

Below is a table showing a few of the most commonly farmed ingredients in this region: -

Category	Ingredient
Legumes	Chickpeas
	Lentils

	Peas
Fruits	Olives
	Mandarin oranges
	Figs
	Grapes
	Lemons
	Persimmons
	Pomegranates
Grains	Barley
	Corn
	Rice
	Wheat
Herbs	Rosemary
	Oregano
	Sage
	Parsley
	Basil
	Dill
	Thyme
	Mint
	Fennel
Nuts	Almonds
	Hazelnuts
	Pine nuts

	Walnuts
Vegetables	Asparagus
	Broccoli
	Cabbage
	Green beans
	Garlic
	Onions
	Eggplant
	Tomatoes
	Broccoli rabe
	Artichokes

Fishing the Mediterranean Sea

The Mediterranean Sea provided a bounty of seafood to the dwellers in that area, and naturally it became an indispensable part of the Mediterranean diet. Fish is rich in omega-3 fatty acids, and hence should be eaten a few times per week to reap all its health benefits. Due to their abundance, one could get sardines, anchovies, octopus, squid, and mackerel for quite cheap back in the day. A few slightly costlier options were mussels, trout, tuna, and clams. Extravagant meals included ingredients like lobster and red mullet.

Today, however, the marine life in the area has gone down significantly due to overfishing, and species vital to the marine ecosystem such as tuna are under threat.

The Mediterranean Way of Life

The healthy Mediterranean way of life is all about eating balanced foods rich in vitamins, minerals, antioxidants, and healthy fatty acids. However, the Mediterranean diet is just one aspect of it. The Mediterranean way of life calls for regular physical exercise, plenty of rest, healthy social interaction, and fun. Balancing all these aspects was the secret of good health of the Mediterranean folk back in the day. However, only the Mediterranean diet is the primary focus of this book, and we will spend most of our time talking about just that.

Eat Healthy Fats

The Mediterranean diet is by no means a low-fat diet, but the fat that is included in this diet is considered healthy for the body, and the heart in particular. Remember: not all fats are created equal. Certain kinds of fats are healthy, while others do more harm than good. Monosaturated fats and polyunsaturated omega-3 fatty acids, for example, are considered healthy. Omegs-6 polyunsaturated fatty acids and saturated fats are unhealthy, and these unhealthy fats are the ones primarily present in most of the common food worldwide. The United States, for example, absolutely loves saturated fats. According to a survey, saturated fats constitute 11% of the total calories of an average American, which is a very high number compared an average Mediterranean resident, who consumes less than 8% of his/her calories through saturated fat. So, if you wish to switch to the healthy Mediterranean way of life, the first thing to do is change the oils you consume. Eliminating fats like butter and lard in favour of healthier oils like olive oil would be the place to start.

Consume Dairy in Moderation

We all love cheese. Dairy products are delicious, nutritious, and great sources of calcium, and should be consumed in moderation if you're following the Mediterranean diet. It is usually a good idea to consume two to three servings of full-fat dairy products in a single day, where one serving can mean an 8-ounce glass of milk, or 8 ounces of yogurt, or an ounce of cheese.

Consume Tons of Plant-Based Foods

As we saw in the pyramid, fruits, vegetables, legumes, and whole grains form the basis of the Mediterranean diet. So, it is a good idea to eat five to ten servings of these in a single day, depending on your appetite. Basically, eat as much of these as you want, but don't overeat. Plant based foods are naturally low in calories, and high in fiber and nutrients. Fresh unprocessed plants are best, so always be on the lookout for the best sources of these around you!

Spice Things Up with Fresh Herbs and Spices

Fresh herbs and Spices are what make most of the recipes insanely delicious, while also providing health benefits. If you already use these in your daily cooking, more power to you! If not, we got you covered!

Consume Seafood Weekly

As we've talked before, one benefit of living close to the sea is the easy access to seafood. However, seafood holds a lower priority than plant-based foods in the Mediterranean diet, and should be consumed in moderation. If you're a vegetarian, consider taking fish oil supplements to get those omega-3 fatty acids into your system. Better yet, considering shunning your vegetarianism, and eating seafood to get the vital nourishment only seafood can provide.

Consume Meat Monthly

Red meat used to be a luxury for the Mediterranean people back in the day. Although not completely off-limits, you should try and reduce your red-meat intake as much as possible. If you absolutely love red meat, consider consuming it no more than two times per month. And even when you do eat it, make sure the serving size of the meat in the dish is small (two to three ounce serving). The main reason to limit meat intake is to limit the amount of unhealthy fats going into your system. As we talked before, saturated fats and omega-6 fatty acids are not good for health, but unfortunately, red meat contains significant quantities of these. As a beef lover myself, I eat a two-ounce serving of it per month, and when I do eat it, I make sure there are lots of vegetables on the side to satiate my hunger.

Drink Wine!

Love wine? Well, it is your lucky day. Having a glass of wine with dinner is a common practice in the Mediterranean regions. Red wine is especially good for the heart and it is a good idea to consume a glass of red wine twice a week. Excess of everything is bad, and wine is no exception so keep it in check. Also, if you're already suffering from health conditions, it is a good idea to check with your doctor before introducing wine to your daily diet.

Work Your Body

Now you don't have to hit the gym like a maniac to work your body. Walking to your destination instead of driving, taking the stairs instead of the lift, or kneading your own dough can all get the job done. So, be creative and work your body when you can. Better yet, play a sport or just hit the gym like a maniac. You don't have to, as I said at the start, but it will help… a lot.

Enjoy a Big Lunch

Lunch was usually the meal of the day when the Mediterranean residents sat with their families and took their time enjoying a big meal. This strengthens social bonds, and relaxes the mind during the most stressful time of the day, when you're just half done with your work, probably.

Have Fun with Friends and Family

Just spending a few minutes per day doing something fun with your loved ones is great for de-stressing. Today, we don't understand the importance of this, and people feel lonely, and in some cases, even depressed. Just doing this one thing has the power to solve a huge chunk of the problems our modern society faces.

Be Passionate

The Mediterranean people are passionate folk. Living on or close to sun-kissed coasts, their passion for life is naturally high. Being passionate about something in life can take you a long way towards health and wellness.

Benefits of the Mediterranean Diet

Now that we have talked about how you can follow the Mediterranean lifestyle, we should talk in detail about all the benefits you will get to reap if you are successful in doing so.

The Diet Fights Free Radicals

The Mediterranean diet is loaded with antioxidants, which help deter the process of oxidation in your body's cells. This reduces the number of free radicals or unstable molecules that cause harm to your cells, tissue, and DNA. In today's world, we have high exposure to harmful elements like vehicle exhaust, industrial waste, water contaminants, toxic foods, etc. These cause the free radicals in the body to escalate, which then increase the risk of chronic diseases of the heart, or even fatal diseases like cancer! Hence, it is absolutely vital to keep these free radicals in check as much as possible, and the best way of doing so naturally is to eat a diet rich in antioxidants, like the Mediterranean diet. The table below shoes a list of antioxidant-rich foods.

Antioxidant	Foods
Vitamin C	Asparagus
	Broccoli
	Cantaloupe
	Cauliflower
	Grapefruit
	Green and red bell peppers
	Guava
	Lemons

	Oranges
	Pineapple
	Strawberries
	Spinach, kale, and collard greens
	Tangerines
	Tomatoes
Vitamin E	Mustard greens, Swiss chard, spinach, and turnip and collard greens
	Almonds
	Peanuts
	Sunflower seeds
Beta carotene	Broccoli
	Cantaloupe
	Carrots
	Cilantro
	Kale, spinach, and turnip and collard greens
	Romaine lettuce

The Diet is Rich in Phytochemicals

We know that plants are rich in vitamins and minerals, but what few of us know is that they are also loaded with chemicals called phytochemicals. These are healthy chemicals contained in plants that provide numerous health benefits to the body, promote heart health, and help prevent certain types of cancers. Ever wondered why different fruits and vegetables exhibit different colours? The reason is the presence of different phytochemicals. Hence, it is possible to tell what kind of phytochemical a plant-based food contains simply by looking at its colour. Refer to the table below to gain some phytochemical knowledge.

Color	Health Benefits	Foods
Blue/purple	A lower risk of some cancers; improved memory; and healthy aging	Blueberries, eggplants, purple grapes, and plums
Green	A lower risk of some cancers; healthy vision; and strong bones and teeth	Broccoli, green peppers, honeydew melon, kiwi, salad greens, and spinach
Red	A lower risk of heart disease and of some cancers, and improved memory function	Pink watermelon, red bell peppers, and strawberries
White	A lower risk of heart disease and of some cancers	Bananas, garlic, and onions
Yellow/orange	A lower risk of heart disease and of some cancers; healthy vision; and a stronger immune system	Carrots, oranges, yellow and orange bell peppers, and yellow watermelon

The Diet is Rich in Vitamin D

The human body gets vitamin D from food sources and from exposure to sunlight. The Mediterranean residents have access to both, and hence have good levels of vitamin D. Some attribute their good health to their high vitamin D levels, and for good reason. Scientific research has demonstrated the numerous health benefits of the vitamin, and a few of these are listed below:

- Guards against Osteoporosis

- Reduces the risk of certain cancers
- Reduces the risk of coronary artery disease
- Reduces vulnerability to common infections such as the common flu

More Healthy Fats in Your Diet

As discussed before, the Mediterranean diet is rich in the healthy monosaturated fats omega-3 polyunsaturated fats, and has lower amounts of unhealthy omega-5 polyunsaturated fats and saturated fats. This has multiple health benefits that include:

- A lower risk of heart disease
- Enhanced insulin function and blood sugar control
- Lower cholesterol levels
- Reduced inflammation in the body
- Body weight management
- Enhanced immune system function
- Management of behavioural issues

More Fiber in Your Diet

It is common knowledge that fiber is great for health. The best sources of fiber are fruits, vegetables, whole grains, and legumes. All of these ingredients are dominant in the Mediterranean diet, and hence by following the Mediterranean diet, you can easily achieve your daily fiber goals. Fiber has multiple benefits for the body, a few of which are listed below:

- Helps maintain a healthy gastrointestinal tract by reducing constipation
- Decreases total cholesterol and bad cholesterol levels, hence promoting heart health
- Reduces the rate at which sugar is absorbed into the blood stream, hence helping maintain healthy blood sugar levels
- Since the body can't break down fiber for energy, it effectively has zero calories, but still fills up the stomach, hence reducing your calorie intake

More Functional Foods in Your Diet

Some foods provide specific health benefits other than basic nutritional benefits. These foods are called functional foods, and they are quite common in the Mediterranean diet. The table below shows the best functional foods to always have in your pantry, along with the benefits they provide.

Food	*Benefits*
Extra-virgin olive oil	Extra-virgin olive oil is loaded with monounsaturated fats and is an excellent source of phytochemicals, including polyphenolic compounds, squalene, and alpha-tocopherol. Health benefits include cardiovascular health, cancer prevention/protection, and immune boosting.
Lemons (zest and juice)	Citrus bioflavonoids benefit both cholesterol and triglycerides. Lemon is also dense source of vitamin C and exhibits anti-inflammatory properties.
Tomatoes and tomato products	Lycopene in tomato products promotes prostate health. Tomato is also a good source of vitamins A and C and carotenoids.
Grapes and grape products (such as red wine)	Phytochemicals in grapes, including polyphenols and resveratrol, promote heart health and brain protection.
Nuts	Nuts are loaded with monounsaturated fats and vitamin E; they also exhibit anti-inflammatory benefits and cardiovascular protection.

Yogurt	Yogurt is a fermented food providing healthy bacteria and healthy fats to your body.
Garlic	Garlic contains allicin, a phytochemical to help manage blood pressure.
Fresh herbs (parsley, basil, oregano, rosemary, and so on)	Herbs loaded with antioxidants and vitamins; plus they contain heart-protective phytosterols. Some herbs are frequently used medicinally.
Olives	Olives are fermented foods providing healthy bacteria to the gut, along with heart-healthy omega-3 fatty acids.
Fatty fish	Fish are rich in omega-3 fatty acids and help reduce triglycerides and inflammation.
Leafy greens	Greens contain phytochemicals such as carotenoids, sulforaphanes, apigenin, and lutein/zeaxanthin. They're cancer protective, immune boosting, vision protective, and heart healthy.
Eggs	Eggs are loaded with vitamin D, lecithin, choline, and lutein/zeaxanthin. Benefits include vision health, brain health, hormone regulation, and bone health.

The Diet Includes Plenty of Pro-Biotic Foods

The human body is home to trillions of health-promoting microbes. These are commonly called "gut bacteria". Research has shown that a good balance of healthy bacteria in your system enhances your immune system, promotes digestion, and even helps with weight loss. The Mediterranean diet includes enough of these pro-biotic foods to make sure a healthy balance of these microbes is always maintained. A few of these pro-biotic foods are- cheese, wine yogurt, sourdough bread, and brined foods such as olives, artichokes, peppers, and capers.

The Diet is Anti-Diabetes

The Mediterranean diet is highly recommended for people with type-2 diabetes because the food in this diet is low on the **Glycaemic Index.** This index is a measure of how fast the carbohydrates in the food break down. If a food scores high on the index, that means that the food breaks down quickly, and causes a sudden spike in blood sugar. Foods low on this index break down slowly and steadily, providing a steady supply of energy to the body, which is healthy.

The Diet is Anti-Aging

The Mediterranean diet can help you feel younger, live longer, and look your best! Here's how the diet accomplishes this:

- **Anti-Disease:** The NIH-AARP Diet and Health Study published in the *Archives of Internal Medicine* in 2007 discovered that people who closely followed a Mediterranean-style diet were 12 to 20 percent less probable to die from cancer and all causes.
- **Anti-Wrinkle:** A study published in the *Journal of the American College of Nutrition* in 2001 discovered that people who followed a diet high in fruits, vegetables, nuts, legumes, and fish exhibited fewer wrinkles on their skin. More research is required on the subject, but you might as well try it out in the meantime.
- **Smoother skin:** The diet is loaded with vitamin C-rich foods, such as oranges, strawberries, and broccoli. These foods lead to higher production of collagen, the skin's support structure.
- **Anti-Inflammation:** Inflammation is an enemy of your heart health, joints, and skin. The Mediterranean diet is loaded with anti-inflammatory foods such as cold-water fish, walnuts, flaxseeds, and fresh herbs, which can help keep you feeling your best.
- **Anti-Alzheimer's:** A 2006 study at Columbia University Medical Center discovered that participants who followed a

Mediterranean-style diet had a 40 percent lower risk of Alzheimer's disease than those who didn't.

- **Forever Young Brain:** Brain structure changes as you age and can cause problems such as memory loss and dementia. According to a 2015 study published in *Neurology*, those who followed a Mediterranean diet, and consumed higher amounts of fish and lower amounts of meat, had less brain atrophy (loss of cells), providing better brain function as they grew older.

The Diet is Anti-Fat

The Mediterranean diet is great if you're looking to lose some weight. But it is even better if you follow the Mediterranean lifestyle while following the diet too. The overall composition of the diet when coupled with physical activity can work wonders!

Planning Your Meals

If you're a beginner and have not yet made the switch to the Mediterranean diet, you will need to identify what changes you need to make to your current diet to make it match closely with the Mediterranean diet. In time, the Mediterranean diet will come to you naturally, but to start off, you will need to plan in advance. You will need to plan your portion sizes, and how often you eat certain foods. The changes are small, but will benefit you in the long run. In this chapter, we will discuss these changes, and basic meal planning.

Importance of Meal Planning

Meal planning is all about creating a road map for what you're going to eat, when you will prepare the food, and what ingredients you will need to buy. It might sound simple, but will save you from a lot of headache, and make your transition to the Mediterranean diet much smoother. Meal planning is vital because:

- It enables you to be efficient with your time

- It enables you to plan what ingredients you will buy and when, so that when you cook them, they are at their freshest
- You don't have to worry about what to cook multiple times per day. You take care of it in one sitting.
- It saves money by reducing food wastage. You cook everything you buy while it is still fresh.

Meal Planning Techniques

Meal planning is a flexible process, and every person has their unique way of going for it. You will eventually discover how you like to plan your meals, but it would be useful to look at a few templates of the common ways of doing it.

- If you like to be moderately thorough and detailed, you can sit down and write what you will eat for breakfast, lunch, and dinner for each day of the week. If you like to munch on snacks from time to time, make sure you write those down too. Make sure the recipes you choose for that week are in season, and you can procure fresh ingredients for the written recipes.
- If you like to get all the thinking for the whole month done in a single sitting, you can prepare meal plans for multiple weeks, along with shopping lists that specify what you will buy, and when, in such a way that the ingredients are at their freshest at the time of cooking. This will take a while, but a good place to start if you have the time. Just make sure you don't plan for too long, and make a new plan with every season so you can get the good seasonal stuff.
- Once you get slightly well acquainted with the diet, you will start to have the Mediterranean staples in your pantry at all times, and you don't need to plan all three meals per day, or even your shopping list. You will have your favourite recipes that you will automatically shuffle as per your convenience. You will start to make larger batches so you can eat leftovers later if you're not in the mood to cook again. You

might need to plan your big dinners once in a while, but that is about it. In a nutshell, Mediterranean cooking will come to you naturally and will require minimal planning.

Sample Summer Meal Plan

Making a meal plan is simple. Just pick a day, and now you have to pick a breakfast, a lunch, and a dinner recipe for that day. Look through the ingredients of each recipe to identify which recipes are in season, and then just pick one. For example, if you're deciding what to eat during a week in summer, you can make a table for each way in the week as follows:

Monday	
Breakfast	Any Breakfast recipe form this book you can prepare on a busy Monday morning during summer. Whip up an oatmeal, or boil a few eggs.
Snack	Any snack recipe from this book that will provide you the energy you need to get through to lunch. If you have leftovers from Sunday, grab those instead.
Lunch	Any big main course recipe from the book that will give you the energy to get through the rest of your workday.
Snack	Any snack recipe from the book to get you to dinner time. If you have leftovers from your previous meals, grab those instead.
Dinner	Any big main course from this book.

Now all you need to do is repeat the process for the rest of the days, and make sure there are at least two seafood recipes in the whole week, and as few meat recipes as possible. Slide a meat recipe in there once every four weeks if you absolutely have to, and even then, keep quantity of the meat small. It really is that simple. I hope you get the idea, and will be able to plan meals at your leisure now.

Buying the Ingredients

If you're used to heading to the market nearest to your home and picking up everything you need from there, you might need to change your habits a little; but only a little. You will still be getting most of your stuff at grocery stores, but you would do well to explore a little, and maybe you will find a few stores that sell fresher products. Below are a few guidelines you will need to follow when shopping for ingredients for the Mediterranean diet:

Shop Local if Possible: Big grocery stores usually source their items from the cheapest possible option they can find, and the cheapest option isn't necessarily the closest one. The farther they source their food from, the longer the food stays in transit, and the less fresh it is. Luckily, regardless of where you live, if you just set out to explore your nearby markets, you will definitely find speciality stores that source or produce their stuff locally. Good luck digging up these hidden gems in your locality! You could also run a google search for such stores, as most of these small stores are now starting to put their locations on google maps.

Local Farmer's Markets are your Friends: I'm not sure about you, but I personally love strolling through a farmer's market, picking out fresh seasonal produce. If you haven't tried it, what are you waiting for? Use the internet to find the nearest farmer's market and get shopping! Visit https://www.localharvest.org/ to find a nearby market if you're in the USA.

Get Into CSA: Community Supported Agriculture is a great way to grab some fresh seasonal produce. All you need to do is pay an upfront fee to a local farm, and in return they will send a box full of fresh produce every week!

More Stores to Look For: Do yourself a favour and look around till you find the best seafood seller, butcher, baker, Mediterranean market, green market, Italian market, or any other place you can get fresh ingredients for your diet.

Setting up Your Pantry

If you're serious about following the Mediterranean diet, you will need to set up your pantry accordingly. The Mediterranean diet has quite a few staple ingredients, and these are used often in the recipes in this book. Let us take a look at a few of these staples that you absolutely have to add to your pantry:

Canned and Dried Beans: Legumes are a staple in the Mediterranean diet, and vital source of protein. They are important ingredients in all kinds of Mediterranean recipes, and hence you will do well to have these on hand at all times. I personally prefer canned beans, but dried beans get the job done too.

Rice and Grains: Rice and grains are also staple ingredients of the Mediterranean diet, and will be used in a large percentage of the recipes in this book. Whole grains are the best. A few of the common grains you will want to keep on hand are: barley, farro, wheat berries, freekeh, and bulgur.

Pasta and Couscous: Pasta is an ingredient in quite a few Mediterranean dishes, and hence should be a staple in your pantry. Whole-wheat pasta is best. Mediterranean dishes also commonly use pearl couscous, which has a slightly bigger grains than regular couscous.

Olives and Olive Oil: Olives and Olive oil are two of the most important ingredients of the Mediterranean diet. When you head to your local market to buy olive oil, make sure you buy quality extra-virgin olive oil. Not all Extra-Virgin Olive Oils (EVOO) are created equal and the brand you choose definitely matters. I've done my fair share of testing in my lifetime, and if you're an American, the California Olive Ranch Everyday Extra Virgin Olive Oil is your best bet. It is quite popular and easily available on amazon.com if you can't find it in a nearby store. This oil is delicious and contains heart-healthy fats as discussed before. Never place olive oil on your kitchen counter, since strong sunlight will cause oxidation of the chlorophyll in the oil, producing stale, harsh flavours. Keeping your olive oil next to the stove is also a bad idea as heat greatly reduces shelf life. It is best to store EVOO in a dark pantry or cupboard; do not store olive oil in the fridge, as it can turn cloudy, thick, and viscous and can take a few hours to revert to normal. You can keep unopened oil for about a year; but once opened, it lasts only about ninety days—so don't buy too much in one go. And if possible, check the harvest date to ensure the freshest bottle possible. If you wish to store the oil in your own container or bottle, make sure it is not clear glass or plastic to reduce the amount of light entering the container/bottle.

When buying olives, it is best to buy unpitted ones, and then pit them later yourself. If, however, you're in a hurry, pre-pitted olives will do the job. To pit olives, start by placing the olives on a flat surface. After that, hold the blade of a knife flat on top of one of the olives. Now, lightly press down on the blade of the knife until the pit pops out. If the pit doesn't pop out all the way, pull it the rest of the way out using your fingers.

Fresh Herbs: Fresh herbs are vital flavouring ingredients in the Mediterranean diet. You will commonly see fresh herbs like mint, oregano, basil, dill, etc. used in the recipes in this book, and hence it is a good idea to keep your pantry stocked with these at all times. These ingredients are also commonly used to garnish the final dish. However, fresh herbs expire quite fast, and need to be stored correctly to make them keep for longer. Lightly wash and then dry your herbs thoroughly by rolling them in paper towels before storing them. These herbs should be placed in airtight bags such as a zipper-lock bag, and these bags should then be placed in the crisper drawer of your fridge.

Dried Herbs: Dried herbs are also a common ingredient in the recipes that follow, and you will do well to make a few of these a staple in your pantry. Rosemary and thyme are the most common dry herbs you should add to your pantry. A few of the recipes will also call for dried mint so make sure you have it before you start preparing a dish that calls for it. Dried herbs keep for longer than fresh ones. Once opened, dried herbs can last for six months to a year, depending on the type of herb. This information is usually provided on the packing. It is quite easy to convert fresh herbs to dry herbs by simply using the microwave. Just microwave them until they appear completely dehydrated. This proves usually takes about one to three minutes. Once dry, allow them to come to room temperature and then store them in a sealed container.

Spices, Spice Blends, and Pastes: Mediterranean dishes use common spices like cinnamon, saffron, paprika, etc. Most of these should be in your pantry already. You will find a few of the recipes in this book that use spices you don't have, and maybe haven't even heard of before, such as sumac, Aleppo pepper, parsley, etc. A few of the recipes in this book will also call for common spice blends and pastes such as:

- North africal Ras El Hanout
- Harissa
- Za'atar

If you can't find these in a nearby store, just buy them online on amazon, or you could prepare these blends on your own. Make sure you store your spices away from heat and light to extend their shelf life.

Cheese, Cured Meats, and Nuts: Feta and Goat cheese are used in a few Mediterranean dishes in this book. Pancetta and Chorizo cured meats and nuts such as almonds and pine are also good to have on hand. When storing cheese, make sure to store it in your fridge after first coating it with a layer or parchment paper, and then with aluminium foil. It is best to store nuts in the freezer, and toast them before using in a recipe.

Yogurt: Although not a heavily used ingredient, a small amount of yogurt is used in quite a few recipes in this book and is hence nice to have on hand. Whole-milk yogurt is obviously best if you're going for the richest possible flavour.

Tahini: Used as a garnish, topping, or a base for sauces, Tahini is made using ground sesame seeds, and is good to have on hand as it is used in quite a few Mediterranean recipes. You can buy this from a nearby store, or online. You can also make your own.

Pomegranate molasses: This is basically dense pomegranate juice. It is used in quite a few Mediterranean recipes, and hence is good to have in your pantry. You can buy this from a nearby store, or online. You can also make your own.

Preserved lemons: Another important ingredient for quite a few Mediterranean dishes that you can buy, or make on your own. These last for several weeks, and are used to add a tangy flavour to the recipes.

Dukkah: It is an Egyptian condiment which is a mix of nuts, seeds, and spices. Make sure you have this with you if you plan to prepare a recipe that calls for it. You can buy this or prepare your own.

Bonus: Snacks and Appetizers

Snacks and appetizers are great to much on while you get to your next big meal. They also serve as a great first course if you're serving a multiple course meal. The Mediterranean diet offers numerous delicious and nutritious antipasti, tapas, meze, and other small plates to choose from. So, without much ado, let us dive into the recipes!

Baba Ghanoush

Yield: Approximately 2 cups

Ⓥ This is a Vegetarian Recipe Ⓥ

Baba ghanoush is a delicious and nutritious meze staple popular in Israel, Lebanon, Palestine, and many other countries!

Ingredients:

- 1 small garlic clove, minced
- 2 eggplants (1 pound each), pricked all over with fork
- 2 tablespoons extra-virgin olive oil, plus extra for serving
- 2 tablespoons tahini
- 2 teaspoons chopped fresh parsley
- 4 teaspoons lemon juice
- Salt and pepper to taste

Directions:

1. Place the oven rack in the centre of the oven and pre-heat your oven to 500 degrees. Place eggplants on a baking sheet coated with aluminium foil and roast, flipping the eggplants every fifteen minutes, until consistently soft when pressed using tongs, forty minutes to one hour. Allow eggplants to cool for 5 minutes over a baking sheet.
2. Place a colander on top of a container. Slice the top and bottom off each eggplant and slit eggplants along the length. Using

spoon, scoop hot pulp into colander (you should have about 2 cups pulp); discard skins. Allow the pulp to drain for about three minutes.

3. Move drained eggplant to your food processor. Put in tahini, oil, lemon juice, garlic, ¾ teaspoon salt, and ¼ teaspoon pepper. Pulse the mixture until a rough puree is achieved, approximately 8 pulses. Drizzle with salt and pepper to taste.

4. Move to serving bowl, cover firmly using plastic wrap, put inside your fridge until chilled, about 1 hour. (Dip will keep safely in a fridge for up to 24 hours; bring to room temperature before you serve.) Drizzle with salt and pepper to taste, sprinkle with extra oil to taste, and drizzle with parsley before you serve.

Brown Feta

Yield: 8 to 12 Servings

This recipe can be made quickly

Ⓥ This is a Vegetarian Recipe Ⓥ

This vegetarian appetizer is for all the Feta lovers out there. Quick and easy to prepare, this recipe tastes great with parsley and olive oil.

Ingredients:

- 2 (8-ounce) blocks feta cheese, sliced into ½-inch-thick slabs
- ¼ teaspoon red pepper flakes
- ¼ teaspoon pepper
- 2 tablespoons extra-virgin olive oil
- 2 teaspoons minced fresh parsley

Directions:

1. Place oven rack 4 inches from broiler element and heat broiler. Pat feta dry using paper towels and lay out on broiler-safe gratin dish.

2. Drizzle with red pepper flakes and pepper. Broil until edges of cheese start to look golden, three to eight minutes. Sprinkle with oil, drizzle with parsley, and serve instantly.

Bruschetta with Artichoke Hearts and Parmesan

Yield: 8 to 10 Servings

This recipe can be made quickly

This is a Vegetarian Recipe

Ingredients:

- 1 cup jarred whole baby artichoke hearts packed in water, rinsed and patted dry
- 1 garlic clove, minced
- 1 recipe Toasted Bread for Bruschetta
- 2 ounces Parmesan cheese, 1 ounce grated fine, 1 ounce shaved
- 2 tablespoons chopped fresh basil
- 2 tablespoons extra-virgin olive oil, plus extra for serving
- 2 teaspoons lemon juice
- Salt and pepper

Directions:

1. Pulse artichoke hearts, oil, basil, lemon juice, garlic, ¼ teaspoon salt, and ¼ teaspoon pepper using a food processor until coarsely pureed, about 6 pulses, scraping down sides of the container as required. Put in grated Parmesan and pulse to combine, about 2 pulses.
2. Lay out artichoke mixture uniformly toasts and top with shaved Parmesan. Season with pepper to taste, and sprinkle with extra oil to taste. Serve.

Bruschetta with Arugula Pesto and Goat Cheese

Yield: 8 to 10 Servings

✗ *This recipe can be made quickly* ✗

Ⓥ *This is a Vegetarian Recipe* Ⓥ

Ingredients:

- ¼ cup extra-virgin olive oil, plus extra for serving
- ¼ cup pine nuts, toasted
- 1 recipe Toasted Bread for Bruschetta
- 1 tablespoon minced shallot
- 1 teaspoon grated lemon zest plus 1 teaspoon juice
- 2 ounces goat cheese, crumbled
- 5 ounces (5 cups) baby arugula
- Salt and pepper

Directions:

1. Pulse arugula, oil, pine nuts, shallot, lemon zest and juice, ½ teaspoon salt, and ¼ teaspoon pepper using a food processor until mostly smooth, approximately 8 pulses, scraping down sides of the container as required.
2. Lay out arugula mixture uniformly toasts, top with goat cheese, and sprinkle with extra oil to taste. Serve.

Bruschetta with Black Olive Pesto, Ricotta, and Basil

Yield: 8 to 10 Servings

✗ *This recipe can be made quickly* ✗

Ingredients:

- ¾ cup pitted kalamata olives
- 1 garlic clove, minced
- 1 recipe Toasted Bread for Bruschetta
- 1 small shallot, minced
- 10 ounces whole-milk ricotta cheese
- 1½ teaspoons lemon juice
- 2 tablespoons extra-virgin olive oil, plus extra for serving
- 2 tablespoons shredded fresh basil
- Salt and pepper

Directions:

1. Pulse olives, shallot, oil, lemon juice, and garlic using a food processor until coarsely chopped, approximately ten pulses, scraping down sides of the container as required. Season ricotta with salt and pepper to taste.
2. Lay out ricotta mixture uniformly toasts, top with olive mixture, and sprinkle with extra oil to taste. Drizzle with basil before you serve.

Bruschetta with Ricotta, Tomatoes, and Basil

Yield: 8 to 10 Servings

✄ *This recipe can be made quickly* ✄

Ⓥ *This is a Vegetarian Recipe* Ⓥ

Ingredients:

- 1 pound cherry tomatoes, quartered
- 1 recipe Toasted Bread for Bruschetta

- 1 tablespoon extra-virgin olive oil, plus extra for serving
- 10 ounces whole-milk ricotta cheese
- 5 tablespoons shredded fresh basil
- Salt and pepper

Directions:

1. Toss tomatoes with 1 teaspoon salt using a colander and allow to drain for about fifteen minutes. Move drained tomatoes to a container, toss with oil and ¼ cup basil, and sprinkle with salt and pepper to taste. In a different container, combine ricotta with remaining 1 tablespoon basil and sprinkle with salt and pepper to taste.
2. Lay out ricotta mixture uniformly toasts, top with tomato mixture, and drizzle lightly with extra oil to taste. Serve.

Caponata

Yield: Approximately 3 cups

Ⓥ This is a Vegetarian Recipe Ⓥ

A delicious and nutritious snack for all eggplant lovers!

Ingredients:

- ¼ cup chopped fresh parsley
- ¼ cup pine nuts, toasted
- ¼ cup raisins
- ¼ cup red wine vinegar, plus extra for seasoning
- ½ teaspoon salt
- ¾ cup V8 juice
- 1 celery rib, chopped fine
- 1 large eggplant (1½ pounds), cut into ½-inch cubes
- 1 large tomato, cored, seeded, and chopped
- 1 red bell pepper, stemmed, seeded, and chopped fine
- 1 small onion, chopped fine (½ cup)

- 1½ teaspoons minced anchovy fillets (2 to 3 fillets)
- 2 tablespoons brown sugar
- 2 tablespoons extra-virgin olive oil
- 2 tablespoons minced black olives

Directions:

1. Toss eggplant with salt in a container. Thoroughly coat the full surface of big microwave-safe plate using double layer of coffee filters and lightly spray using vegetable oil spray. Lay out eggplant in a uniform layer on coffee filters. Microwave until eggplant is dry and shriveled to one-third of its original size, about eight to fifteen minutes (Do not let it brown). Move eggplant instantly to paper towel–lined plate.
2. In the meantime, beat V8 juice, vinegar, sugar, parsley, and anchovies together in medium bowl. Mix in tomato, raisins, and olives.
3. Heat 1 tablespoon oil in 12-inch non-stick frying pan on moderate to high heat until it starts to shimmer. Put in eggplant and cook, stirring intermittently, until edges become browned, about four to eight minutes, adding 1 teaspoon more oil if pan seems to be dry; move to a container.
4. Put in remaining 2 teaspoons oil to now-empty frying pan and heat on moderate to high heat until it starts to shimmer. Put in celery, bell pepper, and onion and cook, stirring intermittently, till they become tender and edges are spotty brown, 6 to 8 minutes.
5. Decrease heat to moderate to low and mix in eggplant and V8 juice mixture. Bring to simmer and cook until V8 juice becomes thick and covers the vegetables, four to eight minutes. Move to serving bowl and allow to cool to room temperature. (Caponata will keep safely in a fridge for up to seven days; bring to room temperature before you serve.)
6. Drizzle with extra vinegar to taste and drizzle with pine nuts before you serve.

Classic Hummus

Yield: Approximately 2 cups

Ⓥ *This is a Vegetarian Recipe* Ⓥ

A popular recipe enjoyed throughout the eastern Mediterranean, Classic Hummus is an easy snack to prepare using simple ingredients!

Ingredients:

- ¼ cup water
- ¼ teaspoon ground cumin
- ½ teaspoon salt
- 1 (15-ounce) can chickpeas, rinsed
- 1 small garlic clove, minced
- 2 tablespoons extra-virgin olive oil, plus extra for serving
- 3 tablespoons lemon juice
- 6 tablespoons tahini
- Pinch cayenne pepper

Directions:

1. Mix water and lemon juice in a small-sized container. In a different container, beat tahini and oil together.
2. Process chickpeas, garlic, salt, cumin, and cayenne using a food processor until thoroughly ground, approximately fifteen seconds.
3. Scrape down sides of the container using a rubber spatula. While the machine runs, put in lemon juice mixture gradually. Scrape down sides of the container and carry on processing for about sixty seconds. While the machine runs, put in tahini mixture gradually and process until hummus is smooth and creamy, approximately fifteen seconds, scraping down sides of the container as required.
4. Move hummus to serving bowl, cover up using plastic wrap, and allow to sit at room temperature until flavours blend, approximately half an hour.
5. If you wish, you can refrigerate this dish for up to 5 days.

6. If needed, loosen hummus using 1 tablespoon warm water. Sprinkle with extra oil to taste before you serve.

Dolmathes

Yield: 24

Ⓥ This is a Vegetarian Recipe Ⓥ

A Greek delicacy, this recipe is basically stuffed grape leaves.

Ingredients:

- ¼ cup chopped fresh mint
- ⅓ cup chopped fresh dill
- ¾ cup short-grain white rice
- 1 (16-ounce) jar grape leaves
- 1 large onion, chopped fine
- 1½ tablespoons grated lemon zest plus 2 tablespoons juice
- 2 tablespoons extra-virgin olive oil, plus extra for serving
- Salt and pepper

Directions:

1. Reserve 24 intact grape leaves, approximately 6 inches in diameter; save for later rest of the leaves. Bring 6 cups water to boil in moderate-sized saucepan. Put in reserved grape leaves and cook for about sixty seconds. Gently drain leaves and move to a container of cold water to cool, about 5 minutes. Drain again, then move leaves to plate and cover loosely using plastic wrap.
2. Heat oil in now-empty saucepan over medium heat until it starts to shimmer. Put in onion and ½ teaspoon salt and cook till they become tender and lightly browned, 5 to 7 minutes. Put in rice and cook, stirring frequently, until grain edges begin to turn translucent, approximately two minutes. Mix in ¾ cup water and bring to boil. Decrease heat to low, cover, and simmer gently until rice becomes soft but still firm in center and water has been

absorbed, 10 to 12 minutes. Remove from the heat, let rice cool slightly, about 10 minutes. Mix in dill, mint, and lemon zest. (Blanched grape leaves and filling will keep safely in a fridge for up to 24 hours.)

3. Place 1 blanched leaf smooth side down on counter with stem facing you. Get rid of the stem from base of leaf by slicing along both sides of stem to form thin triangle. Pat leaf dry using paper towels. Overlap cut ends of leaf to stop any filling from leaking out. Place heaping tablespoon filling ¼ inch from bottom of leaf where ends overlap. Fold bottom over filling and fold in sides. Roll leaf tightly around filling to create tidy roll. Replicate the process with the rest of the blanched leaves and filling.

4. Line 12-inch frying pan with one layer of remaining leaves. Place rolled leaves seam side down in tight rows in prepared skillet. Mix 1¼ cups water and lemon juice, put in to skillet, and bring to simmer over medium heat. Cover, decrease the heat to moderate to low, and simmer until water is almost completely absorbed and leaves and rice are tender and cooked through, forty to sixty minutes.

5. Move stuffed grape leaves to serving platter and allow to cool to room temperature, approximately half an hour; discard leaves in skillet. Sprinkle with extra oil before you serve.

Easy Toasted Almonds

Yield: 2 cups

This recipe can be made quickly

Ⓥ This is a Vegetarian Recipe Ⓥ

Meze platters are a delicious part of the Mediterranean diet, and toasted nuts are a vital part of it.

Ingredients:

- ¼ teaspoon pepper

- 1 tablespoon extra-virgin olive oil
- 1 teaspoon salt
- 2 cups skin-on raw whole almonds

Directions:

1. Heat oil in 12-inch non-stick frying pan on moderate to high heat until it barely starts shimmering. Put in almonds, salt, and pepper and decrease the heat to moderate to low. Cook, stirring frequently, until almonds become aromatic and their colour becomes somewhat deep, approximately eight minutes.
2. Move almonds to plate coated using paper towels and allow to cool before you serve.
3. If you wish, you can store Almonds at room temperature for up to 5 days.

Fiery Red Whipped Feta

Yield: Approximately 2 cups

This recipe can be made quickly

Ⓥ This is a Vegetarian Recipe Ⓥ

The Greeks call this recipe "htipiti". This simple dish tastes great and is super quick and easy to make.

Ingredients:

- ¼ teaspoon pepper
- ⅓ cup extra-virgin olive oil, plus extra for serving
- ½ teaspoon cayenne pepper
- 1 cup jarred roasted red peppers, rinsed, patted dry, and chopped
- 1 tablespoon lemon juice
- 8 ounces feta cheese, crumbled (2 cups)

Directions:

1. Process feta, red peppers, oil, lemon juice, cayenne, and pepper using a food processor until smooth, approximately half a minute, scraping down sides of the container as required.
2. Move mixture to serving bowl, sprinkle with extra oil to taste, and serve. (Dip will keep safely in a fridge for up to 2 days; bring to room temperature before you serve.)

Flavourful Calamari with Oranges

Yield: 6 to 8 Servings

An aromatic snack from Fance!

Ingredients:

- ¼ cup extra-virgin olive oil
- ⅓ cup hazelnuts, toasted, skinned, and chopped
- 1 red bell pepper, stemmed, seeded, and cut into 2-inch-long matchsticks
- 1 shallot, sliced thin
- 1 teaspoon Dijon mustard
- 2 celery ribs, sliced thin on bias
- 2 garlic cloves, minced
- 2 oranges
- 2 pounds squid, bodies sliced crosswise into ¼-inch-thick rings, tentacles halved
- 2 tablespoons baking soda
- 2½ tablespoons harissa
- 3 tablespoons chopped fresh mint
- 3 tablespoons red wine vinegar
- Salt and pepper

Directions:

1. Dissolve baking soda and 1 tablespoon salt in 3 cups cold water in large container. Submerge squid in brine, cover, put inside

your fridge for about fifteen minutes. Remove squid from brine and separate bodies from tentacles.

2. Bring 8 cups water to boil in a big saucepan on moderate to high heat. Fill big container with ice water. Put in 2 tablespoons salt and tentacles to boiling water and cook for 30 seconds. Put in bodies and cook until bodies are firm and opaque throughout, about 90 seconds. Drain squid, move to ice water, and allow to sit until chilled, about 5 minutes.

3. Beat oil, vinegar, harissa, garlic, mustard, 1½ teaspoons salt, and ½ teaspoon pepper together in a big container. Drain squid well and put in to a container with dressing.

4. Cut away peel and pith from oranges. Quarter oranges, then slice crosswise into ½-inch-thick pieces. Put in oranges, bell pepper, celery, and shallot to squid and toss to coat. Cover and put in the fridge for minimum sixty minutes or up to 24 hours. Mix in hazelnuts and mint and sprinkle with salt and pepper to taste before you serve.

Flavourful Green-Black Olives

Yield: 8 Servings

Ⓥ *This is a Vegetarian Recipe* Ⓥ

Why buy marinated olives from a store when you can create a much more delicious version of the snack right at home?

Ingredients:

- ½ teaspoon red pepper flakes
- ½ teaspoon salt
- ¾ cup extra-virgin olive oil
- 1 cup brine-cured black olives with pits
- 1 cup brine-cured green olives with pits
- 1 garlic clove, minced
- 1 shallot, minced
- 2 teaspoons grated lemon zest

- 2 teaspoons minced fresh oregano
- 2 teaspoons minced fresh thyme

Directions:

1. Wash olives comprehensively, then drain and pat dry using paper towels.
2. Toss olives with the rest of the ingredients in a container, cover, put inside your fridge for minimum 4 hours or for maximum 4 days. Allow to sit at room temperature for minimum half an hour before you serve.

Flavourful Saffron Caulipeas

Yield: 6 to 8 Servings

Ⓥ *This is a Vegetarian Recipe* Ⓥ

Marinated chickpeas and cauliflower taste absolutely amazing with saffron!

Ingredients:

- ⅛ teaspoon saffron threads, crumbled
- ⅓ cup extra-virgin olive oil
- ½ head cauliflower (1 pound), cored and cut into 1-inch florets
- ½ lemon, sliced thin
- 1 cup canned chickpeas, rinsed
- 1 small sprig fresh rosemary
- 1 tablespoon minced fresh parsley
- 1½ teaspoons smoked paprika
- 1½ teaspoons sugar
- 2 tablespoons sherry vinegar
- 5 garlic cloves, peeled and smashed
- Salt and pepper

Directions:

1. Bring 2 quarts water to boil in a big saucepan. Put in cauliflower and 1 tablespoon salt and cook until florets start to become tender, approximately three minutes. Drain florets and move to paper towel–lined baking sheet.
2. Mix ¼ cup hot water and saffron in a container; set aside. Heat oil and garlic in small saucepan over moderate to low heat until aromatic and starting to sizzle but not brown, four to eight minutes. Mix in sugar, paprika, and rosemary and cook until aromatic, approximately half a minute. Remove from the heat, mix in saffron mixture, vinegar, 1½ teaspoons salt, and ¼ teaspoon pepper.
3. Mix florets, saffron mixture, chickpeas, and lemon in a big container. Cover and place in the fridge, stirring intermittently, for minimum 4 hours or for maximum 3 days. To serve, discard rosemary sprig, move cauliflower and chickpeas to serving bowl using a slotted spoon, and drizzle with parsley.

Garmary White Bean Dip

Yield: Approximately 1¼ cups

✔ This recipe can be made quickly ✔

Ⓥ *This is a Vegetarian Recipe* Ⓥ

White beans are a staple ingredient in Mediterranean cuisines from Turkey to Tuscany. These beans are smooth and taste delicious!

Ingredients:

- ¼ cup extra-virgin olive oil
- 1 (15-ounce) can cannellini beans, rinsed
- 1 small garlic clove, minced
- 1 teaspoon minced fresh rosemary
- 2 tablespoons water
- 2 teaspoons lemon juice
- Pinch cayenne pepper

- Salt and pepper

Directions:

1. Process beans, 3 tablespoons oil, water, lemon juice, rosemary, garlic, ¼ teaspoon salt, ¼ teaspoon pepper, and cayenne using a food processor until smooth, approximately fifty seconds, scraping down sides of the container as required.
2. Move to serving bowl, cover up using plastic wrap, and allow to sit at room temperature until flavours blend, approximately half an hour.
3. (Dip will keep safely in a fridge for up to 24 hours; if needed, loosen dip using 1 tablespoon warm water before you serve.) Drizzle with salt and pepper to taste and drizzle with residual 1 tablespoon oil before you serve.

Giardiniera

Yield: four 1-pint jars

Ⓥ This is a Vegetarian Recipe Ⓥ

Love the taste of pickles? Try this Italian veggie delight.

Ingredients:

- ¼ cup sugar
- ½ head cauliflower (1 pound), cored and cut into ½-inch florets
- 1 cup chopped fresh dill
- 1 red bell pepper, stemmed, seeded, and cut into ½-inch-wide strips
- 2 serrano chiles, stemmed and sliced thin
- 2 tablespoons salt
- 2¼ cups water
- 2¾ cups white wine vinegar
- 3 carrots, peeled and sliced ¼ inch thick on bias
- 3 celery ribs, cut crosswise into ½-inch pieces

- 4 garlic cloves, sliced thin

Directions:

1. Mix cauliflower, carrots, celery, bell pepper, serranos, and garlic in a big container, then move to four 1-pint jars with tight-fitting lids.
2. Bundle dill in cheesecloth and tie using a kitchen twine to secure. Bring dill sachet, vinegar, water, sugar, and salt to boil in a big saucepan on moderate to high heat. Turn off the heat and allow to steep for about ten minutes. Discard dill sachet.
3. Return brine to brief boil, then pour uniformly over vegetables. Allow it to cool to room temperature, then cover put inside your fridge until vegetables taste pickled, minimum 7 days or maximum 1 month.

Infused Artichokes

Yield: 6 to 8 Servings

Ⓥ This is a Vegetarian Recipe Ⓥ

Marinated Artichokes taste absolutely amazing and can be thrown on pretty much everything.

Ingredients:

- ¼ teaspoon red pepper flakes
- 2 lemons
- 2 sprigs fresh thyme
- 2 tablespoons minced fresh mint
- 2½ cups extra-virgin olive oil
- 3 pounds baby artichokes (2 to 4 ounces each)
- 8 garlic cloves, peeled, 6 cloves smashed, 2 cloves minced
- Salt and pepper

Directions:

1. Take a vegetable peeler and use it to remove three 2-inch strips zest from 1 lemon. Grate ½ teaspoon zest from second lemon and set aside. Halve and juice lemons to yield ¼ cup juice, saving the spent lemon halves for later.
2. Mix oil and lemon zest strips in a big saucepan. Working with 1 artichoke at a time, cut top quarter off each artichoke, eliminate the outer leaves, and slice off any dark parts. Peel and trim stem, then cut artichoke in half along the length (quarter artichoke if large). Rub each artichoke half with previously saved spent lemon half and put in saucepan.
3. Put in smashed garlic, pepper flakes, thyme sprigs, 1 teaspoon salt, and ¼ teaspoon pepper to saucepan and quickly bring to simmer on high heat. Decrease heat to moderate to low and simmer, stirring intermittently to submerge all artichokes, until artichokes can be pierced with fork but are still firm, about 5 minutes. Remove from heat, cover, and allow to sit until artichokes are fork-tender and fully cooked, approximately twenty minutes.
4. Gently mix in ½ teaspoon reserved grated lemon zest, ¼ cup reserved lemon juice, and minced garlic. Move artichokes and oil to serving bowl and allow to cool to room temperature. Drizzle with salt to taste and drizzle with mint. Serve. (Artichokes and oil will keep safely in a fridge for up to 4 days.)

Labneh

Yield: Approximately 1 cup

Ⓥ This is a Vegetarian Recipe Ⓥ

Basically, this recipe is strained yogurt with its whey removed, making it a delicious, thick, rich, and tangy delicacy. It is highly popular in eastern Mediterranean regions.

Ingredients:

- 2 cups plain yogurt

Directions:

1. Cover fine-mesh strainer using 3 basket-style coffee filters or double layer of cheesecloth. Set strainer over big measuring vessel with plenty of room on the bottom.
2. Spoon yogurt into strainer, cover firmly using plastic wrap, put inside your fridge until yogurt has discharged approximately one cup liquid and has creamy, cream cheese–like texture, minimum 10 hours or for maximum 2 days.
3. Move drained yogurt to a clean bowl; discard liquid. Serve. (Yogurt will keep safely in a fridge for up to 2 days.)

Lavash Crackers

Yield: 10 to 12 Servings

Ⓥ *This is a Vegetarian Recipe* Ⓥ

This crispy eastern Mediterranean snack will taste great with a dip of your choice!

Ingredients:

- ⅓ cup extra-virgin olive oil, plus extra for brushing
- ¾ cup (3¾ ounces) all-purpose flour
- ¾ cup (4⅛ ounces) whole-wheat flour
- ¾ teaspoon salt
- 1 cup warm water
- 1 large egg, lightly beaten
- 1 teaspoon coarsely ground pepper
- 1½ cups (8⅝ ounces) semolina flour
- 2 tablespoons sesame seeds
- 2 teaspoons sea salt or kosher salt

Directions:

1. Use a stand mixer with a dough hook attachment to combine semolina flour, whole-wheat flour, all-purpose flour, and salt

together on low speed. Progressively put in water and oil and knead until dough is smooth and elastic, seven to nine minutes. Turn dough out onto slightly floured counter and knead using your hands to form smooth, round ball. Split the dough into 4 equivalent pieces, brush with oil, and cover up using plastic wrap. Allow to rest at room temperature for about one hour.

2. Place two oven racks in your oven one just above, and one just below the middle position and pre-heat your oven to 425 degrees. Slightly coat two 18 by 13-inch rimless (or inverted) baking sheets using vegetable oil spray.

3. Work with two pieces of dough at a time while keeping the rest covered in plastic. Press dough into small rectangles, then move to the readied sheets. Using rolling pin and hands, roll and stretch dough uniformly to edges of sheet. Using fork, make holes in doughs at 2-inch gaps. Brush doughs with beaten egg, then drizzle each with 1½ teaspoons sesame seeds, ½ teaspoon salt, and ¼ teaspoon pepper. Push lightly on seasonings to help them stick.

4. Bake crackers until a deep golden brown colour is achieved, fifteen to twenty minutes, switching and rotating sheets halfway through baking. Move crackers to wire rack and allow to cool fully. Allow the baking sheets to cool to room temperature before rolling out and baking the rest of the dough. Break cooled lavash into big crackers and serve. (Lavash can be stored safely at room temperature for up to 2 weeks.)

Muhammara

Yield: Approximately 2 cups

This recipe can be made quickly

This is a Vegetarian Recipe

A delicious Syrian delicacy that goes swimmingly with any vegetable dish.

Ingredients:

- ⅛ teaspoon cayenne pepper
- ¼ cup plain wheat crackers, crumbled
- ½ teaspoon ground cumin
- ¾ teaspoon salt
- 1 cup walnuts, toasted
- 1 tablespoon minced fresh parsley (optional)
- 1½ cups jarred roasted red peppers, rinsed and patted dry
- 2 tablespoons extra-virgin olive oil
- 3 tablespoons pomegranate molasses
- Lemon juice, as required

Directions:

1. Pulse all ingredients except parsley using a food processor until smooth, approximately ten pulses. Move to serving bowl, cover, put inside your fridge for about fifteen minutes. (Dip will keep safely in a fridge for up to 24 hours; bring to room temperature before you serve.)
2. Drizzle with lemon juice, salt, and cayenne to taste and drizzle with parsley, if using, before you serve.

Mussels Escabèche

Yield: 6 to 8 Servings

This aromatic briny snack is goof for any occasion!

Ingredients:

- ¼ cup sherry vinegar
- ⅓ cup extra-virgin olive oil
- ½ small red onion, sliced ¼ inch thick
- ⅔ cup water
- ⅔ cup white wine
- ¾ teaspoon smoked paprika
- 2 bay leaves
- 2 pounds mussels, scrubbed and debearded

- 2 sprigs fresh thyme
- 2 tablespoons minced fresh parsley
- 4 garlic cloves, sliced thin
- Salt and pepper

Directions:

1. Bring wine and water to boil in Dutch oven on high heat. Put in mussels, cover, and cook, stirring intermittently, until mussels open, 3 to 6 minutes. Strain mussels and discard cooking liquid and any mussels that have not opened. Let mussels cool slightly, then remove mussels from shells and place in a big container; discard shells.
2. Heat oil in now-empty Dutch oven over medium heat until it starts to shimmer. Put in onion, garlic, bay leaves, thyme, 1 tablespoon parsley, and paprika. Cook, stirring frequently, until garlic is aromatic and onion is slightly wilted, about 1 minute.
3. Remove from the heat, mix in vinegar, ¼ teaspoon salt, and ⅛ teaspoon pepper. Pour mixture over mussels and allow to sit for about fifteen minutes. (Mussels will keep safely in a fridge for up to 2 days; bring to room temperature before you serve.) Drizzle with salt and pepper to taste and drizzle with remaining 1 tablespoon parsley before you serve.

Olive Oil–Sea Salt Pita Chips

Yield: 8 Servings

✗ *This recipe can be made quickly* ✗

Ⓥ *This is a Vegetarian Recipe* Ⓥ

Ingredients:

- ½ cup extra-virgin olive oil
- 1 teaspoon sea salt or kosher salt
- 4 (8-inch) pita breads

Directions:

1. Place two oven racks in your oven one just above, and one just below the middle position and pre-heat your oven to 350 degrees. Using kitchen shears, slice around perimeter of each pita and divide into 2 thin rounds.
2. Work with the rounds one at a time, and brush rough side heavily with oil and season with salt. Stack rounds one over the other, rough side up, as you go. Take a chef's knife and slice pita stack into 8 wedges. Lay out wedges, rough side up and in one layer, on 2 rimmed baking sheets.
3. Bake until wedges start to look golden brown and crisp, about fifteen minutes, rotating and switching sheets halfway through baking. Allow it to cool before you serve. (Pita chips can be stored safely at room temperature for up to 3 days.)

Packed Sardines

Yield: 8 Servings

Sardines make a scrumptious seafood snack.

Ingredients:

- ¼ cup golden raisins, chopped fine
- ¼ cup pine nuts, toasted and chopped fine
- ⅓ cup capers, rinsed and minced
- ⅓ cup panko bread crumbs
- 2 garlic cloves, minced
- 2 tablespoons minced fresh parsley
- 2 teaspoons grated orange zest plus wedges for serving
- 3 tablespoons extra-virgin olive oil
- 8 fresh sardines (2 to 3 ounces each), scaled, gutted, head and tail on
- Salt and pepper

Directions:

1. Place oven rack to lower-middle position and pre-heat your oven to 450 degrees. Coat rimmed baking sheet using aluminium foil. Mix capers, raisins, pine nuts, 1 tablespoon oil, parsley, orange zest, garlic, ¼ teaspoon salt, and ¼ teaspoon pepper in a container. Put in panko and slowly mix until blended.
2. Use a pairing knife to slit belly of fish open from gill to tail, leaving spine undamaged. Gently rinse fish under cold running water and pat dry using paper towels. Rub skin of sardines evenly with remaining 2 tablespoons oil and sprinkle with salt and pepper.
3. Place sardines on readied sheet, spaced 1 inch apart. Stuff cavities of each sardine with 2 tablespoons filling and push on filling to help it stick; softly press fish closed.
4. Bake until fish flakes apart when softly poked using paring knife and filling is golden brown, about fifteen minutes. Serve with orange wedges.

Provençal Anchovy Dip

Yield: Approximately 1½ cups

A flavourful dip to go with vegetables!

Ingredients:

- ¼ cup extra-virgin olive oil, plus extra for serving
- ¼ cup water
- ¾ cup whole blanched almonds
- 1 garlic clove, minced
- 1 tablespoon minced fresh chives
- 1 teaspoon Dijon mustard
- 2 tablespoons lemon juice, plus extra for serving
- 2 tablespoons raisins
- 20 anchovy fillets (1½ ounces), rinsed, patted dry, and minced
- Salt and pepper

Directions:

1. Bring 4 cups water to boil in moderate-sized saucepan on moderate to high heat. Put in almonds and cook till they become tender, approximately twenty minutes. Drain and wash thoroughly.
2. Process drained almonds, anchovies, water, raisins, lemon juice, garlic, mustard, ¼ teaspoon pepper, and ⅛ teaspoon salt using a food processor until a somewhat smooth paste is achieved, approximately two minutes, scraping down sides of the container as required. While your food processor runs slowly put in oil and process to smooth puree, approximately two minutes.
3. Move mixture to a container, mix in 2 teaspoons chives, and sprinkle with salt and extra lemon juice to taste. (Dip will keep safely in a fridge for up to 2 days; bring to room temperature before you serve.) Drizzle with the rest of the chives and extra oil to taste before you serve.

Rich Turkish Nut Dip

Yield: Approximately 1 cup

This recipe can be made quickly

Ⓥ This is a Vegetarian Recipe Ⓥ

A delicious and nutritious ultra-smooth dip from Turkey!

Ingredients:

- ¼ cup extra-virgin olive oil
- ¾ cup water, plus extra as required
- 1 cup blanched almonds, blanched hazelnuts, pine nuts, or walnuts, toasted
- 1 slice hearty white sandwich bread, crusts removed, torn into 1-inch pieces
- 1 small garlic clove, minced

- 2 tablespoons lemon juice, plus extra as required
- Pinch cayenne pepper
- Salt and pepper

Directions:

1. Using a fork, mash bread and water together in a container till it turns into a paste. Process bread mixture, nuts, oil, lemon juice, garlic, ½ teaspoon salt, ⅛ teaspoon pepper, and cayenne using a blender until smooth, approximately two minutes. Put in extra water as required until sauce is slightly thicker than consistency of heavy cream.
2. Drizzle with salt, pepper, and extra lemon juice to taste. Serve at room temperature. (Sauce will keep safely in a fridge for up to 2 days; bring to room temperature before you serve.)

Searing Garlic Shrimp

Yield: 8 Servings

A Mediterranean classic, shrimp and garlic go hand in hand.

Ingredients:

- ¼ teaspoon salt
- ½ cup extra-virgin olive oil
- 1 (2-inch) piece mild dried chile, approximately broken, with seeds
- 1 bay leaf
- 1 pound medium-large shrimp (31 to 40 per pound), peeled, deveined, and tails removed
- 1 tablespoon minced fresh parsley
- 1½ teaspoons sherry vinegar
- 14 garlic cloves, peeled, 2 cloves minced, 12 cloves left whole

Directions:

1. Toss shrimp with minced garlic, 2 tablespoons oil, and salt in a container and allow to marinate at room temperature for minimum half an hour or maximum 1 hour.
2. In the meantime, use the flat side of a chef's knife to smash 4 garlic cloves. Heat smashed garlic and remaining 6 tablespoons oil in 12-inch frying pan over moderate to low heat, stirring intermittently, until garlic is light golden brown, four to eight minutes; allow the oil to cool to room temperature. Using slotted spoon, take out and discard smashed garlic.
3. Finely cut remaining 8 garlic cloves. Return frying pan with cooled oil to low heat and put in sliced garlic, bay leaf, and chile. Cook, stirring intermittently, until garlic becomes soft but not browned, four to eight minutes. If garlic does not begun to sizzle after 3 minutes, raise the heat to moderate to low.
4. Increase heat to moderate to low and put in shrimp with marinade. Cook, without stirring, until oil starts to bubble mildly, approximately two minutes. Using tongs, flip shrimp and carry on cooking until almost cooked through, approximately two minutes. Increase heat to high and put in vinegar and parsley. Cook, stirring continuously, until shrimp are cooked through and oil is bubbling heavily, 15 to 20 seconds. Take out and throw away the bay leaf. Serve instantly.

Skordalia

Yield: Approximately 2 cups

Ⓥ This is a Vegetarian Recipe Ⓥ

A thick garlic dip from Greece that tastes sensational with seafood and vegetables!

Ingredients:

- ¼ cup extra-virgin olive oil
- ¼ cup plain Greek yogurt

- 1 (10- to 12-ounce) russet potato, peeled and cut into 1-inch chunks
- 2 slices hearty white sandwich bread, crusts removed, torn into 1-inch pieces
- 3 garlic cloves, minced to paste
- 3 tablespoons lemon juice
- 6 tablespoons warm water, plus extra as required
- Salt and pepper

Directions:

1. Place potato in small saucepan and put in water to cover by 1 inch. Bring water to boil, then decrease heat to simmer and cook until potato becomes soft and paring knife can be inserted into potato easily, fifteen to twenty minutes. Drain potato using a colander, tossing to eliminate all surplus water.
2. In the meantime, combine garlic and lemon juice in a container and allow to sit for about ten minutes. In separate medium bowl, mash bread, ¼ cup warm water, and ½ teaspoon salt till it turns into a paste with fork.
3. Move potato to ricer (food mill fitted with small disk) and process into a container with bread mixture. Mix in lemon-garlic mixture, oil, yogurt, and remaining 2 tablespoons warm water until thoroughly mixed. (Sauce will keep safely in a fridge for up to 3 days; bring to room temperature before you serve.) Drizzle with salt and pepper to taste and adjust consistency with extra warm water as required before you serve.

Soft and Crispy Halloumi

Yield: 6 to 8 Servings

⚡ This recipe can be made quickly ⚡

Ⓥ *This is a Vegetarian Recipe* Ⓥ

Soft on the inside, and crispy on the outside, this recipe makes for a great first course.

Ingredients:

- 1 (8-ounce) block halloumi cheese, sliced into ½-inch-thick slabs
- 1 tablespoon all-purpose flour
- 2 tablespoons cornmeal
- 2 tablespoons extra-virgin olive oil
- Lemon wedges

Directions:

1. Mix cornmeal and flour in shallow dish. Working with 1 piece of cheese at a time, coat both wide sides with cornmeal mixture, pressing to help coating stick; move to plate.
2. Heat oil in 12-inch non-stick frying pan over medium heat until it starts to shimmer. Arrange halloumi in one layer in frying pan and cook until golden brown on both sides, 2 to 4 minutes each side. Move to platter and serve with lemon wedges.

Stuffed Dates Wrap

Yield: 6 to 8 Servings

This recipe can be made quickly

This one snack has a wide spectrum of flavours! What are the flavours? Only one way to find out!

Ingredients:

- ½ cup minced fresh parsley
- ½ teaspoon grated orange zest
- ⅔ cup walnuts, toasted and chopped fine
- 12 large pitted dates, halved along the length
- 12 thin slices prosciutto, halved along the length
- 2 tablespoons extra-virgin olive oil

- Salt and pepper

Directions:

1. Mix walnuts, parsley, oil, and orange zest in a container and sprinkle with salt and pepper to taste. Mound 1 large teaspoon filling into centre of each date half.
2. Wrap prosciutto tightly around dates. Serve. (Dates will keep safely in a fridge for up to 8 hours; bring to room temperature before you serve.)

Toasted Bread for Bruschetta

Yield: 8 to 10 Servings

This recipe can be made quickly

Ⓥ This is a Vegetarian Recipe Ⓥ

Ingredients:

- 1 (10 by 5-inch) loaf country bread with thick crust, ends discarded, sliced crosswise into ¾-inch-thick pieces
- 1 garlic clove, peeled
- Extra-virgin olive oil
- Salt

Directions:

1. Toast the bread immediately before assembling the bruschetta.
2. Place oven rack 4 inches from broiler element and heat broiler. Place bread on a baking sheet coated with an aluminium foil.
3. Broil until bread becomes deeply golden and toasted on both sides, 1 to 2 minutes each side. Lightly rub 1 side of each toast with garlic. Brush with oil and sprinkle with salt to taste.

Tzatziki

Yield: Approximately 2 cups

Ⓥ This is a Vegetarian Recipe Ⓥ

Tzatziki is a classic Greek sauce made out of strained yogurt and cucumber, and can be enjoyed as a dip for raw vegetables, or dolloped over grilled meat of your choice.

Ingredients:

- 1 (12-ounce) cucumber, peeled, halved along the length, seeded, and shredded
- 1 cup whole-milk Greek yogurt
- 1 small garlic clove, minced
- 2 tablespoons extra-virgin olive oil
- 2 tablespoons minced fresh mint and/or dill
- Salt and pepper

Directions:

1. Toss cucumber with ½ teaspoon salt using a colander and allow to drain for about fifteen minutes.
2. Beat yogurt, oil, mint, and garlic together in a container, then combine in the drained cucumber. Cover and put in the fridge until chilled, minimum sixty minutes or up to 2 days. Drizzle with salt and pepper to taste before you serve.

Bonus: Soups

Soups go well before a big meal. Go ahead and try these delicious and nutritious soups!

Artichoke-Mushroom Soup

Yield: 4 to 6 Servings

Artichokes, mushrooms, and root vegetables taste great together in s soup!

Ingredients:

- ¼ cup dry white wine
- ¼ cup heavy cream
- 1 leek, white and light green parts only, halved along the length, sliced ¼ inch thick, and washed thoroughly
- 1 teaspoon minced fresh thyme or ¼ teaspoon dried
- 1 teaspoon white wine vinegar, plus extra for seasoning
- 12 ounces white mushrooms, trimmed and sliced thin
- 2 anchovy fillets, rinsed, patted dry, and minced
- 2 bay leaves
- 2 tablespoons minced fresh tarragon
- 3 cups chicken broth
- 3 cups jarred whole baby artichokes packed in water, quartered, rinsed, and patted dry
- 3 cups vegetable broth
- 3 tablespoons all-purpose flour
- 3 tablespoons extra-virgin olive oil
- 4 garlic cloves, minced
- 6 ounces parsnips, peeled and cut into ½-inch pieces
- Salt and pepper

Directions:

1. Heat 1 tablespoon oil in Dutch oven on moderate heat until it starts to shimmer. Put in artichokes and cook until browned, eight to ten minutes. Move to slicing board, allow to cool slightly, then chop coarse.
2. Heat 1 tablespoon oil in now-empty pot on moderate heat until it starts to shimmer. Put in mushrooms, cover, and cook until they have released their liquid, approximately five minutes. Uncover and carry on cooking until mushrooms are dry, approximately five minutes.
3. Mix in leek and residual 1 tablespoon oil and cook until leek is softened and mushrooms become browned, eight to ten

minutes. Mix in garlic, anchovies, and thyme and cook until aromatic, approximately half a minute. Mix in flour and cook for about sixty seconds. Mix in wine, scraping up any browned bits, and cook until nearly evaporated, about 1 minute.

4. Slowly beat in chicken broth and vegetable broth, smoothing out any lumps. Mix in artichokes, parsnips, and bay leaves and bring to simmer. Decrease heat to low, cover, and simmer gently until parsnips are tender, fifteen to twenty minutes. Remove from the heat, discard bay leaves. Mix in cream, tarragon, and vinegar. Drizzle with salt, pepper, and extra vinegar to taste. Serve.

Classic Chicken Broth

Yield: Approximately 8 cups

Chicken broth is a timeless classic, almost all over the planet.

Ingredients:

- 1 onion, chopped
- 14 cups water
- 2 bay leaves
- 2 teaspoons salt
- 4 pounds chicken backs and wings

Directions:

1. Heat chicken and water in big stockpot or Dutch oven on moderate to high heat until boiling, skimming off any scum that comes to surface. Decrease heat to low and simmer slowly for three hours.
2. Put in onion, bay leaves, and salt and continue to simmer for another 2 hours.
3. Strain broth through fine-mesh strainer into a big container, pressing on solids to extract as much liquid as possible. Allow broth to settle for approximately five minutes, then skim off fat.

(Cooled broth will keep safely in a fridge for maximum 4 days or frozen for maximum 1 month.)

Classic Croutons

Yield: Approximately 3 cups

This recipe can be made quickly

Ⓥ This is a Vegetarian Recipe Ⓥ

Got some stale bread lying around you want to get rid of? This recipe will get the job done.

Ingredients:

- 3 tablespoons extra-virgin olive oil
- 6 slices hearty white sandwich bread, crusts removed, cut into ½-inch cubes (3 cups)
- Salt and pepper

Directions:

1. Place the oven rack in the centre of the oven and pre-heat your oven to 350 degrees. Toss bread with oil, sprinkle with salt and pepper, and spread in rimmed baking sheet. Bake until a golden brown colour is achieved and it becomes crunchy, 20 minutes to half an hour, stirring halfway through baking.
2. Allow it to cool and serve. (Croutons can be stored safely at room temperature for up to 3 days.)

Classic Gazpacho

Yield: 8 to 10 Servings

Ⓥ This is a Vegetarian Recipe Ⓥ

A refreshing cold chilli tomato soup popular in southern Spain!

Ingredients:

- ⅓ cup sherry vinegar
- ½ small sweet onion or 2 large shallots, chopped fine
- 1 teaspoon hot sauce (optional)
- 1½ pounds tomatoes, cored and cut into ¼-inch pieces
- 2 garlic cloves, minced
- 2 red bell peppers, stemmed, seeded, and cut into ¼-inch pieces
- 2 small cucumbers (1 peeled, both sliced along the length, seeded, and cut into ¼-inch pieces)
- 5 cups tomato juice
- 8 ice cubes
- Extra-virgin olive oil
- Salt and pepper

Directions:

1. Mix tomatoes, bell peppers, cucumbers, onion, vinegar, garlic, and 2 teaspoons salt in a big container (at least 4-quart) and season with pepper to taste. Allow to stand until vegetables barely start to discharge their juices, approximately five minutes. Mix in tomato juice, ice cubes, and hot sauce, if using. Cover and put in the fridge to blend flavours, minimum 4 hours or for maximum 2 days.
2. Scoop out and throw away any ice cubes that remain, and sprinkle soup with salt and pepper to taste. Pour into your soup bowls, drizzle with oil, and serve.

Cold Cucumber-Yogurt Soup

Yield: 6 Servings

Ⓥ *This is a Vegetarian Recipe* Ⓥ

A fresh-tasting chilled soup popular in Turkey and Greece.

Ingredients:

- ¼ teaspoon sugar
- 1 tablespoon lemon juice
- 1½ tablespoons minced fresh dill
- 1½ tablespoons minced fresh mint
- 2 cups plain Greek yogurt
- 2 cups water
- 4 scallions, green parts only, chopped coarse
- 5 pounds English cucumbers, peeled and seeded (1 cucumber cut into ½-inch pieces, remaining cucumbers cut into 2-inch pieces)
- Extra-virgin olive oil
- Salt and pepper

Directions:

1. Toss 2-inch pieces of cucumber with scallions. Working in 2 batches, process cucumber-scallion mixture using a blender with water until smoothened thoroughly, approximately two minutes; move to big container. Beat in yogurt, lemon juice, 1½ teaspoons salt, sugar, and pinch pepper. Cover and put in the fridge to combine the flavours, minimum sixty minutes or maximum 12 hours.
2. Mix in dill and mint and sprinkle with salt and pepper to taste. Serve, topped with remaining ½-inch pieces of cucumber and drizzled with oil.

Fiery Moroccan Chicken Lentil Soup

Yield: 8 Servings

Ingredients:

- ¼ cup harissa, plus extra for serving
- ¼ teaspoon cayenne pepper
- ¼ teaspoon ground cinnamon
- ⅓ cup minced fresh cilantro
- ½ teaspoon paprika
- ¾ cup green or brown lentils, picked over and rinsed

- 1 (15-ounce) can chickpeas, rinsed
- 1 onion, chopped fine
- 1 tablespoon all-purpose flour
- 1 tablespoon extra-virgin olive oil
- 1 teaspoon grated fresh ginger
- 1 teaspoon ground cumin
- 10 cups chicken broth
- 1½ pounds bone-in split chicken breasts, trimmed
- 4 plum tomatoes, cored and cut into ¾-inch pieces
- Pinch saffron threads, crumbled
- Salt and pepper

Directions:

1. Pat chicken dry using paper towels and sprinkle with salt and pepper. Heat oil in Dutch oven on moderate to high heat until just smoking. Brown chicken lightly, approximately three minutes each side; move to plate.
2. Put in onion to fat left in pot and cook on moderate heat till they become tender, approximately five minutes. Mix in ginger, cumin, paprika, cinnamon, cayenne, ¼ teaspoon pepper, and saffron and cook until aromatic, approximately half a minute. Mix in flour and cook for about sixty seconds. Slowly beat in broth, scraping up any browned bits and smoothing out any lumps, and bring to boil.
3. Mix in lentils and chickpeas, then nestle chicken into pot and bring to simmer. Cover, decrease the heat to low, and simmer gently until chicken registers 160 degrees, fifteen to twenty minutes.
4. Move chicken to slicing board, allow to cool slightly, then shred into bite-size pieces using 2 forks, discarding skin and bones. In the meantime, continue to simmer lentils, covered, for 25 to 30 minutes.
5. Mix in shredded chicken and cook until heated through, approximately two minutes. Mix in tomatoes, cilantro, and harissa and sprinkle with salt and pepper to taste. Serve, passing extra harissa separately.

French Lentil Soup

Yield: 4 to 6 Servings

Ingredients:

- ½ cup dry white wine
- 1 (14.5-ounce) can diced tomatoes, drained
- 1 bay leaf
- 1 cup lentilles du Puy, picked over and rinsed
- 1 large onion, chopped fine
- 1 teaspoon minced fresh thyme or ¼ teaspoon dried
- 1½ cups water
- 1½ teaspoons balsamic vinegar
- 2 carrots, peeled and chopped
- 3 garlic cloves, minced
- 3 slices bacon, cut into ¼-inch pieces
- 3 tablespoons minced fresh parsley
- 4½ cups chicken broth, plus extra as required
- Salt and pepper

Directions:

1. Cook bacon in Dutch oven on moderate to high heat, stirring frequently, until crisp, approximately five minutes. Mix in onion and carrots and cook until vegetables start to become tender, approximately two minutes. Mix in garlic and thyme and cook until aromatic, approximately half a minute. Mix in tomatoes and bay leaf and cook until aromatic, approximately half a minute. Mix in lentils and ¼ teaspoon salt. Cover, decrease the heat to moderate to low, and cook until vegetables are softened and lentils have darkened, eight to ten minutes.
2. Increase heat to high, mix in wine, and bring to simmer. Mix in broth and water and bring to boil. Partially cover pot, decrease the heat to low, and simmer gently until lentils are tender but still hold their shape, 30 to 35 minutes.

3. Discard bay leaf. Process 3 cups soup using a blender until smooth, approximately half a minute, then return to pot. Heat soup gently over low heat until hot (do not boil) and adjust consistency with extra hot broth as required. Mix in vinegar and parsley and sprinkle with salt and pepper to taste. Serve.

Greek White Bean Soup

Yield: 6 Servings

Ⓥ This is a Vegetarian Recipe Ⓥ

Ingredients:

- 1 onion, chopped
- 1 pound (2½ cups) dried cannellini beans, picked over and rinsed
- 1 teaspoon ground dried Aleppo pepper
- 2 tablespoons chopped fresh parsley
- 2 tablespoons extra-virgin olive oil, plus extra for serving
- 2½ teaspoons minced fresh oregano or ¾ teaspoon dried
- 3 tablespoons lemon juice
- 4 celery ribs, cut into ½-inch pieces
- 6 cups chicken or vegetable broth, plus extra as required
- Salt and pepper

Directions:

1. Dissolve 3 tablespoons salt in 4 quarts cold water in large container. Put in beans and soak at room temperature for minimum 8 hours or for maximum 24 hours. Drain and wash thoroughly.
2. Heat oil in Dutch oven on moderate heat until it starts to shimmer. Put in onion, ½ teaspoon salt, and ½ teaspoon pepper and cook till they become tender and lightly browned, 5 to 7 minutes. Mix in oregano and cook until aromatic, approximately half a minute. Mix in broth, celery, and soaked beans and bring

to boil. Decrease heat to low, cover, and simmer until beans are tender, 45 to 60 minutes.

3. Process 2 cups soup using a blender until smooth, approximately half a minute, then return to pot. Heat soup gently over low heat until hot (do not boil) and adjust consistency with extra hot broth as required. Mix in lemon juice, Aleppo, and parsley and sprinkle with salt and pepper to taste. Serve, drizzling individual portions with extra oil.

Green Pea Soup

Yield: 6 Servings

Ingredients:

QUICK PEA BROTH

- 1 carrot, chopped
- 1 garlic clove, lightly crushed
- 1 small onion, chopped
- 1 teaspoon salt
- 1¾ cups chicken broth
- 2 bay leaves
- 6 cups water
- 8 ounces snow peas, chopped

SOUP

- ½ cup dry white wine
- 1 cup Arborio rice
- 1 garlic clove, minced
- 1 onion, chopped fine
- 1½ ounces Parmesan cheese, grated (¾ cup)
- 2 ounces pancetta, chopped fine
- 2 tablespoons extra-virgin olive oil
- 2 teaspoons lemon juice
- 20 ounces frozen peas

- 4 teaspoons minced fresh parsley
- Salt and pepper

Directions:

1. FOR THE QUICK PEA BROTH Mix all ingredients in Dutch oven and bring to boil on moderate to high heat. Decrease heat to moderate to low, partially cover, and simmer for 30 minutes. Strain broth through fine-mesh strainer into moderate-sized saucepan, pressing on solids with wooden spoon to extract as much liquid as possible. Cover and keep warm over low heat until ready to use.
2. FOR THE SOUP Heat oil in now-empty pot on moderate heat until it starts to shimmer. Put in onion and pancetta and cook, stirring intermittently, until onion is softened and lightly browned, 5 to 7 minutes. Mix in garlic and cook until aromatic, approximately half a minute. Put in rice and cook, stirring often, until grain edges begin to turn translucent, approximately three minutes.
3. Put in wine and cook, stirring continuously, until fully absorbed, about 1 minute. Mix in warm broth and bring to boil. Decrease heat to moderate to low, cover, and simmer, stirring intermittently, until rice is just cooked, about fifteen minutes. Mix in peas and cook until heated through, approximately two minutes. Remove from the heat, mix in Parmesan, parsley, and lemon juice and sprinkle with salt and pepper to taste. Serve instantly.

Italian Pasta e Fagioli

Yield: 8 to 10 Servings

Ingredients:

- ¼ cup minced fresh parsley
- ¼ teaspoon red pepper flakes
- ½ teaspoon fennel seeds
- 1 (28-ounce) can diced tomatoes

- 1 celery rib, minced
- 1 cup orzo
- 1 fennel bulb, stalks discarded, bulb halved, cored, and chopped fine
- 1 onion, chopped fine
- 1 Parmesan cheese rind, plus grated Parmesan for serving
- 1 tablespoon extra-virgin olive oil, plus extra for serving
- 1 tablespoon minced fresh oregano or 1 teaspoon dried
- 2 (15-ounce) cans cannellini beans, rinsed
- 2 teaspoons grated orange zest
- 2½ cups water
- 3 anchovy fillets, rinsed and minced
- 3 ounces pancetta, chopped fine
- 3½ cups chicken broth
- 4 garlic cloves, minced
- Salt and pepper

Directions:

1. Heat oil in Dutch oven on moderate to high heat until it starts to shimmer. Put in pancetta and cook, stirring intermittently, until starting to brown, 3 to 5 minutes. Mix in onion, fennel, and celery and cook until vegetables are softened, 5 to 7 minutes. Mix in garlic, anchovies, oregano, orange zest, fennel seeds, and pepper flakes and cook until aromatic, about 1 minute.
2. Mix in tomatoes and their juice, scraping up any browned bits. Mix in Parmesan rind and beans, bring to simmer, and cook until flavours blend, about 10 minutes.
3. Mix in broth, water, and 1 teaspoon salt. Increase heat to high and bring to boil. Mix in pasta and cook until al dente, about 10 minutes. Remove from the heat, discard Parmesan rind. Mix in parsley and sprinkle with salt and pepper to taste. Serve, drizzling individual portions with extra oil and sprinkling with grated Parmesan.

Libyan Lamb-Mint Sharba

Yield: 6 to 8 Servings

Ingredients:

- ¼ teaspoon ground cumin
- ½ teaspoon ground cinnamon
- 1 (15-ounce) can chickpeas, rinsed
- 1 cup orzo
- 1 onion, chopped fine
- 1 pound lamb shoulder chops (blade or round bone), 1 to 1½ inches thick, trimmed and halved
- 1 tablespoon extra-virgin olive oil
- 1 teaspoon ground turmeric
- 1 teaspoon paprika
- 10 cups chicken broth
- 1½ teaspoons dried mint, crumbled
- 2 tablespoons tomato paste
- 4 plum tomatoes, cored and cut into ¼-inch pieces
- Salt and pepper

Directions:

1. Place oven rack to lower-middle position and pre-heat your oven to 325 degrees. Pat lamb dry using paper towels and sprinkle with salt and pepper. Heat oil in Dutch oven on moderate to high heat until just smoking. Brown lamb, about 4 minutes each side; move to plate. Pour off all but 2 tablespoons fat from pot.
2. Put in onion to fat left in pot and cook on moderate heat till they become tender, approximately five minutes. Mix in tomatoes and cook till they become tender and juice has evaporated, approximately two minutes. Mix in tomato paste, 1 teaspoon mint, turmeric, paprika, 1 teaspoon salt, cinnamon, cumin, and ¼ teaspoon pepper and cook until aromatic, about 1 minute. Mix in broth, scraping up any browned bits, and bring to boil.

3. Mix in chickpeas, then nestle lamb into pot along with any accumulated juices. Cover, place pot in oven, and cook until fork slips easily in and out of lamb, about 1 hour.

4. Move lamb to slicing board, allow to cool slightly, then shred into bite-size pieces using 2 forks, discarding excess fat and bones. In the meantime, stir orzo into soup, bring to simmer on moderate heat, and cook until tender, 10 to 12 minutes.

5. Mix in shredded lamb and cook until heated through, approximately two minutes. Remove from the heat, mix in remaining ½ teaspoon mint and allow to sit until aromatic, about 1 minute. Serve.

Moroccan Chickpea Soup

Yield: 4 to 6 Servings

Ⓥ *This is a Vegetarian Recipe* Ⓥ

Ingredients:

- ¼ cup minced fresh parsley or mint
- ¼ teaspoon ground cumin
- ¼ teaspoon ground ginger
- ¼ teaspoon saffron threads, crumbled
- ½ teaspoon hot paprika
- 1 (14.5-ounce) can diced tomatoes
- 1 onion, chopped fine
- 1 pound red potatoes, unpeeled, cut into ½-inch pieces
- 1 teaspoon sugar
- 1 zucchini, cut into ½-inch pieces
- 2 (15-ounce) cans chickpeas, rinsed
- 3 tablespoons extra-virgin olive oil
- 3½ cups chicken or vegetable broth
- 4 garlic cloves, minced
- Lemon wedges
- Salt and pepper

Directions:

1. Heat oil in Dutch oven on moderate to high heat until it starts to shimmer. Put in onion, sugar, and ½ teaspoon salt and cook until onion is softened, approximately five minutes. Mix in garlic, paprika, saffron, ginger, and cumin and cook until aromatic, approximately half a minute. Mix in chickpeas, potatoes, tomatoes and their juice, zucchini, and broth. Bring to simmer and cook, stirring intermittently, until potatoes are tender, 20 to 30 minutes.

2. Using wooden spoon, mash some of potatoes against side of pot to thicken soup. Remove from the heat, mix in parsley and sprinkle with salt and pepper to taste. Serve with lemon wedges.

Moroccan Spicy Fava Bean Soup

Yield: 4 to 6 Servings

Ⓥ *This is a Vegetarian Recipe* Ⓥ

Ingredients:

- ¼ cup lemon juice (2 lemons)
- 1 onion, chopped
- 1 pound (3 cups) dried split fava beans, picked over and rinsed
- 2 cups water
- 2 teaspoons cumin, plus extra for serving
- 2 teaspoons paprika, plus extra for serving
- 3 tablespoons extra-virgin olive oil, plus extra for serving
- 5 garlic cloves, minced
- 6 cups chicken or vegetable broth, plus extra as required
- Salt and pepper

Directions:

1. Heat oil in Dutch oven on moderate heat until it starts to shimmer. Put in onion, ¾ teaspoon salt, and ¼ teaspoon pepper

and cook till they become tender and lightly browned, 5 to 7 minutes. Mix in garlic, paprika, and cumin and cook until aromatic, approximately half a minute.

2. Mix in beans, broth, and water and bring to boil. Cover, decrease the heat to low, and simmer gently, stirring intermittently, until beans are soft and broken down, 1½ to 2 hours.

3. Remove from the heat, beat soup heavily until broken down to coarse puree, approximately half a minute. Adjust consistency with extra hot broth as required. Mix in lemon juice and sprinkle with salt and pepper to taste. Serve, drizzling individual portions with extra oil and sprinkling with extra paprika and cumin.

Provençal Vegetable Soup

Yield: 6 Servings

Ⓥ *This is a Vegetarian Recipe* Ⓥ

This is a timeless French soup made with seasonal vegetables, creamy white beans, and aromatic herbs.

Ingredients:

PISTOU

- ⅓ cup extra-virgin olive oil
- ½ cup fresh basil leaves
- 1 garlic clove, minced
- 1 ounce Parmesan cheese, grated (½ cup)

SOUP

- ½ cup orecchiette
- 1 (15-ounce) can cannellini or navy beans, rinsed
- 1 carrot, peeled and sliced ¼ inch thick
- 1 celery rib, cut into ½-inch pieces
- 1 large tomato, cored, seeded, and chopped

- 1 leek, white and light green parts only, halved along the length, sliced ½ inch thick, and washed thoroughly
- 1 small zucchini, halved along the length, seeded, and cut into ¼-inch pieces
- 1 tablespoon extra-virgin olive oil
- 2 garlic cloves, minced
- 3 cups vegetable broth
- 3 cups water
- 8 ounces haricots verts, trimmed and cut into ½-inch lengths
- Salt and pepper

Directions:

1. **For the Pistou**: Process all ingredients using a food processor until smooth, approximately fifteen seconds, scraping down sides of the container as required. (Pistou will keep safely in a fridge for maximum 4 hours.)
2. **For the Soup**: Heat oil in Dutch oven on moderate heat until it starts to shimmer. Put in leek, celery, carrot, and ½ teaspoon salt and cook until vegetables are softened, eight to ten minutes. Mix in garlic and cook until aromatic, approximately half a minute. Mix in broth and water and bring to simmer.
3. Mix in pasta and simmer until slightly softened, approximately five minutes. Mix in haricots verts and simmer until bright green but still crunchy, approximately three minutes. Mix in cannellini beans, zucchini, and tomato and simmer until pasta and vegetables are tender, approximately three minutes. Drizzle with salt and pepper to taste. Serve, topping individual portions with pistou.

Provene Fish Soup

Yield: 6 to 8 Servings

Ingredients:

- ⅛ teaspoon red pepper flakes

- 1 cup dry white wine or dry vermouth
- 1 fennel bulb, 2 tablespoons fronds minced, stalks discarded, bulb halved, cored, and cut into ½-inch pieces
- 1 onion, chopped
- 1 tablespoon extra-virgin olive oil, plus extra for serving
- 1 tablespoon grated orange zest
- 1 teaspoon paprika
- 2 (8-ounce) bottles clam juice
- 2 bay leaves
- 2 celery ribs, halved along the length and cut into ½-inch pieces
- 2 pounds skinless hake fillets, 1 to 1½ inches thick, sliced crosswise into 6 equivalent pieces
- 2 tablespoons minced fresh parsley
- 4 cups water
- 4 garlic cloves, minced
- 6 ounces pancetta, chopped fine
- Pinch saffron threads, crumbled
- Salt and pepper

Directions:

1. Heat oil in Dutch oven on moderate heat until it starts to shimmer. Put in pancetta and cook, stirring intermittently, until starting to brown, 3 to 5 minutes. Mix in fennel pieces, onion, celery, and 1½ teaspoons salt and cook until vegetables are softened and lightly browned, 12 to 14 minutes. Mix in garlic, paprika, pepper flakes, and saffron and cook until aromatic, approximately half a minute.
2. Mix in wine, scraping up any browned bits. Mix in water, clam juice, and bay leaves. Bring to simmer and cook until flavours blend, fifteen to twenty minutes.
3. Remove from the heat, discard bay leaves. Nestle hake into cooking liquid, cover, and allow to sit until fish flakes apart when softly poked using paring knife and registers 140 degrees, eight to ten minutes. Gently mix in parsley, fennel fronds, and orange zest and break fish into large pieces. Drizzle with salt and pepper to taste. Serve, drizzling individual portions with extra oil.

Red Pepper Roast Soup with Sides

Yield: 6 Servings

Ⓥ *This is a Vegetarian Recipe* Ⓥ

Roasted red peppers bring a rich smoky flavour to the soup.

Ingredients:

- ½ cup half-and-half
- ½ cup whole-milk yogurt
- ½ teaspoon ground cumin
- ½ teaspoon smoked paprika
- 1 bay leaf
- 1 red onion, chopped
- 1 tablespoon all-purpose flour
- 1 tablespoon extra-virgin olive oil
- 1 teaspoon lime juice
- 2 garlic cloves, minced
- 2 tablespoons dry sherry
- 2 tablespoons tomato paste
- 3 tablespoons minced fresh cilantro
- 4 cups chicken or vegetable broth, plus extra as required
- 8 red bell peppers, cored and flattened
- Salt and pepper

Directions:

1. Beat yogurt, 1 tablespoon cilantro, and lime juice together in a container. Drizzle with salt and pepper to taste. Cover and put in the fridge until needed.
2. Place oven rack 3 inches from broiler element and heat broiler. Lay out half of peppers skin side up on a baking sheet coated with an aluminium foil. Broil until skin is charred and puffed but flesh is still firm, eight to ten minutes, rotating sheet halfway through broiling. Move broiled peppers to a container, cover up

using plastic wrap or foil, and let steam until skins peel off easily, 10 to fifteen minutes. Replicate the process with the rest of the peppers. Peel broiled peppers, discarding skins, and chop coarse.

3. Cook oil and garlic together in Dutch oven over low heat, stirring continuously, until garlic is foamy, sticky, and straw-colored, six to eight minutes. Mix in onion and ¼ teaspoon salt, increase heat to medium, and cook till they become tender, approximately five minutes.

4. Mix in cumin and paprika and cook until aromatic, approximately half a minute. Mix in tomato paste and flour and cook for about sixty seconds. Slowly beat in broth, scraping up any browned bits and smoothing out any lumps. Mix in bay leaf and chopped peppers, bring to simmer, and cook until peppers are very tender, 5 to 7 minutes.

5. Discard bay leaf. Working in batches, process soup using a blender until smooth, approximately two minutes. Return soup to clean pot and mix in half-and-half and sherry. Heat soup gently over low heat until hot (do not boil) and adjust consistency with extra hot broth as required. Mix in remaining 2 tablespoons cilantro and sprinkle with salt and pepper to taste. Serve, drizzling individual portions with yogurt mixture.

Shellfish Soup

Yield: 6 to 8 Servings

Ingredients:

- ⅛ teaspoon red pepper flakes
- ⅓ cup minced fresh parsley
- ½ teaspoon ground turmeric
- 1 cup dry white wine or dry vermouth
- 1 teaspoon grated fresh ginger
- 1 teaspoon ground coriander
- 1½ pounds leeks, white and light green parts only, halved along the length, sliced thin, and washed thoroughly

- 12 ounces large sea scallops, tendons removed
- 12 ounces large shrimp (26 to 30 per pound), peeled and deveined, shells reserved
- 12 ounces squid, bodies sliced crosswise into ½-inch-thick rings, tentacles halved
- 2 (8-ounce) bottles clam juice
- 2 garlic cloves, minced
- 2 tablespoons extra-virgin olive oil, plus extra for serving
- 3 tablespoons tomato paste
- 4 cups water
- 4 ounces pancetta, chopped fine
- Salt and pepper

Directions:

1. Heat 1 tablespoon oil in Dutch oven on moderate heat until it starts to shimmer. Put in shrimp shells and cook, stirring often, until starting to turn spotty brown and pot starts to brown, 2 to 4 minutes. Put in wine and simmer, stirring intermittently, for 2 minutes. Mix in water, bring to simmer, and cook for 4 minutes. Strain mixture through fine-mesh strainer into a container, pressing on solids to extract as much liquid as possible; discard solids.

2. Heat residual 1 tablespoon oil in now-empty pot on moderate heat until it starts to shimmer. Put in leeks and pancetta and cook until leeks are softened and lightly browned, approximately eight minutes. Mix in tomato paste, garlic, 1 teaspoon salt, ginger, coriander, turmeric, and pepper flakes and cook until aromatic, about 1 minute. Mix in wine mixture and clam juice, scraping up any browned bits. Bring to simmer and cook until flavours blend, fifteen to twenty minutes.

3. Decrease heat to gentle simmer, put in sea scallops, and cook for 2 minutes. Mix in shrimp and cook until just opaque throughout, approximately two minutes. Remove from the heat, mix in squid, cover, and allow to sit until just opaque and tender, 1 to 2 minutes. Mix in parsley and sprinkle with salt and pepper to taste. Serve, drizzling individual portions with extra oil.

Sicilian Chickpea-Escarole Soup

Yield: 6 to 8 Servings

Ⓥ This is a Vegetarian Recipe Ⓥ

Ingredients:

- ¼ teaspoon red pepper flakes
- 1 (3-inch) strip orange zest
- 1 head escarole (1 pound), trimmed and cut into 1-inch pieces
- 1 large tomato, cored and chopped
- 1 Parmesan cheese rind, plus grated Parmesan for serving
- 1 pound (2¾ cups) dried chickpeas, picked over and rinsed
- 1 small onion, chopped
- 2 bay leaves
- 2 fennel bulbs, stalks discarded, bulbs halved, cored, and chopped fine
- 2 tablespoons extra-virgin olive oil, plus extra for serving
- 2 teaspoons minced fresh oregano or ½ teaspoon dried
- 5 cups chicken or vegetable broth
- 5 garlic cloves, minced
- Salt and pepper

Directions:

1. Dissolve 3 tablespoons salt in 4 quarts cold water in large container. Put in chickpeas and soak at room temperature for minimum 8 hours or for maximum 24 hours. Drain and wash thoroughly.
2. Heat oil in Dutch oven on moderate heat until it starts to shimmer. Put in fennel, onion, and 1 teaspoon salt and cook until vegetables are softened, 7 to 10 minutes. Mix in garlic, oregano, and pepper flakes and cook until aromatic, approximately half a minute.

3. Mix in 7 cups water, broth, soaked chickpeas, Parmesan rind, bay leaves, and orange zest and bring to boil. Reduce to gentle simmer and cook until chickpeas are tender, 1¼ to 1¾ hours.

4. Mix in escarole and tomato and cook until escarole is wilted, 5 to 10 minutes. Remove from the heat, discard bay leaves and Parmesan rind (scraping off any cheese that has melted and adding it back to pot). Drizzle with salt and pepper to taste. Serve, drizzling individual portions with extra oil and sprinkling with grated Parmesan.

Spanish Lentil-Chorizo Soup

Yield: 6 to 8 Servings

Ingredients:

- ⅛ teaspoon ground cloves
- 1 large onion
- 1 pound (2¼ cups) lentils, picked over and rinsed
- 1 tablespoon all-purpose flour
- 1½ pounds Spanish-style chorizo sausage, pricked with fork several times
- 2 bay leaves
- 2 tablespoons sweet smoked paprika
- 3 carrots, peeled and cut into ¼-inch pieces
- 3 garlic cloves, minced
- 3 tablespoons minced fresh parsley
- 3 tablespoons sherry vinegar, plus extra for seasoning
- 5 tablespoons extra-virgin olive oil
- Salt and pepper

Directions:

1. Place lentils and 2 teaspoons salt in heatproof container. Cover with 4 cups boiling water and let soak for 30 minutes. Drain well.

2. In the meantime, finely chop three-quarters of onion (you should have about 1 cup) and grate remaining quarter (you should have

about 3 tablespoons). Heat 2 tablespoons oil in Dutch oven on moderate heat until it starts to shimmer. Put in chorizo and cook until browned on all sides, six to eight minutes. Move chorizo to large plate. Decrease heat to low and put in chopped onion, carrots, 1 tablespoon parsley, and 1 teaspoon salt. Cover and cook, stirring intermittently, until vegetables are very soft but not brown, 25 to 30 minutes. If vegetables begin to brown, put in 1 tablespoon water to pot.

3. Put in lentils and vinegar to vegetables, increase heat to medium-high, and cook, stirring often, until vinegar starts to evaporate, three to five minutes. Put in 7 cups water, chorizo, bay leaves, and cloves; bring to simmer. Decrease heat to low; cover; and cook until lentils are tender, approximately half an hour.

4. Heat remaining 3 tablespoons oil in small saucepan on moderate heat until it starts to shimmer. Put in paprika, grated onion, garlic, and ½ teaspoon pepper; cook, stirring continuously, until aromatic, 2 minutes. Put in flour and cook, stirring continuously, 1 minute longer. Remove chorizo and bay leaves from lentils. Stir paprika mixture into lentils and carry on cooking until flavors have blended and soup has thickened, 10 to fifteen minutes. When chorizo is cool enough to handle, cut in half along the length, then cut each half into ¼-inch-thick slices. Return chorizo to soup along with remaining 2 tablespoons parsley and heat through, about 1 minute. Drizzle with salt, pepper, and up to 2 teaspoons vinegar to taste and serve. (Soup can be made up to 3 days in advance.)

Spanish Meatball-Saffron Soup

Yield: 6 to 8 Servings

Ingredients:

MEATBALLS

- ⅓ cup whole milk

- ½ teaspoon pepper
- ½ teaspoon salt
- 1 ounce Manchego cheese, grated (½ cup)
- 1 shallot, minced
- 2 slices hearty white sandwich bread, torn into quarters
- 2 tablespoons extra-virgin olive oil
- 3 tablespoons minced fresh parsley
- 8 ounces 80 percent lean ground beef
- 8 ounces ground pork

SOUP

- ⅛ teaspoon red pepper flakes
- ¼ teaspoon saffron threads, crumbled
- 1 cup dry white wine
- 1 onion, chopped fine
- 1 recipe Picada
- 1 red bell pepper, stemmed, seeded, and cut into ¾-inch pieces
- 1 tablespoon extra-virgin olive oil
- 1 teaspoon paprika
- 2 garlic cloves, minced
- 2 tablespoons minced fresh parsley
- 8 cups chicken broth
- Salt and pepper

Directions:

1. FOR THE MEATBALLS Using fork, mash bread and milk together till it turns into a paste in a big container. Mix in ground pork, Manchego, parsley, shallot, oil, salt, and pepper until combined. Put in ground beef and knead with your hands until combined. Pinch off and roll 2-teaspoon-size pieces of mixture into balls and lay out on rimmed baking sheet (you should have 30 to 35 meatballs). Cover using plastic wrap put inside your fridge until firm, minimum 30 minutes.

2. FOR THE SOUP Heat oil in large Dutch oven on moderate to high heat until it starts to shimmer. Put in onion and bell pepper and cook till they become tender and lightly browned, eight to ten

minutes. Mix in garlic, paprika, saffron, and pepper flakes and cook until aromatic, approximately half a minute. Mix in wine, scraping up any browned bits, and cook until almost completely evaporated, about 1 minute.

3. Mix in broth and bring to simmer. Gently put in meatballs and simmer until cooked through, 10 to 12 minutes. Remove from the heat, mix in picada and parsley and sprinkle with salt and pepper to taste. Serve.

Spicy Moroccan Lamb Lentil Soup

Yield: 6 to 8 Servings

Ingredients:

- ¼ cup harissa, plus extra for serving
- ¼ teaspoon cayenne pepper
- ¼ teaspoon ground cinnamon
- ⅓ cup minced fresh cilantro
- ½ teaspoon paprika
- ¾ cup green or brown lentils, picked over and rinsed
- 1 (15-ounce) can chickpeas, rinsed
- 1 onion, chopped fine
- 1 pound lamb shoulder chops (blade or round bone), 1 to 1½ inches thick, trimmed and halved
- 1 tablespoon all-purpose flour
- 1 tablespoon extra-virgin olive oil
- 1 teaspoon grated fresh ginger
- 1 teaspoon ground cumin
- 10 cups chicken broth
- 4 plum tomatoes, cored and cut into ¾-inch pieces
- Pinch saffron threads, crumbled
- Salt and pepper

Directions:

1. Place oven rack to lower-middle position and pre-heat your oven to 325 degrees. Pat lamb dry using paper towels and sprinkle with salt and pepper. Heat oil in Dutch oven on moderate to high heat until just smoking. Brown lamb, about 4 minutes each side; move to plate. Pour off all but 2 tablespoons fat from pot.
2. Put in onion to fat left in pot and cook on moderate heat till they become tender, approximately five minutes. Mix in ginger, cumin, paprika, cinnamon, cayenne, ¼ teaspoon pepper, and saffron and cook until aromatic, approximately half a minute. Mix in flour and cook for about sixty seconds. Slowly beat in broth, scraping up any browned bits and smoothing out any lumps, and bring to boil.
3. Nestle lamb into pot along with any accumulated juices, bring to simmer, and cook for about ten minutes. Mix in lentils and chickpeas, cover, and place pot in oven. Cook until fork slips easily in and out of lamb and lentils are tender, fifty to sixty minutes.
4. Move lamb to slicing board, allow to cool slightly, then shred into bite-size pieces using 2 forks, discarding excess fat and bones. Stir shredded lamb into soup and allow to sit until heated through, approximately two minutes. Mix in tomatoes, cilantro, and harissa and sprinkle with salt and pepper to taste. Serve, passing extra harissa separately.

Spicy Red Lentil Soup

Yield: 4 to 6 Servings

Ⓥ This is a Vegetarian Recipe Ⓥ

Ingredients:

- ⅛ teaspoon ground cinnamon
- ¼ cup chopped fresh cilantro
- ¼ cup extra-virgin olive oil
- ¼ teaspoon ground ginger

- ½ teaspoon ground cumin
- ¾ teaspoon ground coriander
- 1 garlic clove, minced
- 1 large onion, chopped fine
- 1 tablespoon tomato paste
- 1 teaspoon paprika
- 10½ ounces (1½ cups) red lentils, picked over and rinsed
- 1½ teaspoons dried mint, crumbled
- 2 cups water
- 2 tablespoons lemon juice, plus extra for seasoning
- 4 cups chicken or vegetable broth, plus extra as required
- Pinch cayenne pepper
- Salt and pepper

Directions:

1. Heat 2 tablespoons oil in a big saucepan on moderate heat until it starts to shimmer. Put in onion and 1 teaspoon salt and cook, stirring intermittently, till they become tender, approximately five minutes. Mix in coriander, cumin, ginger, cinnamon, ¼ teaspoon pepper, and cayenne and cook until aromatic, approximately two minutes. Mix in tomato paste and garlic and cook for about sixty seconds.
2. Mix in broth, water, and lentils and bring to vigorous simmer. Cook, stirring intermittently, until lentils are soft and about half are broken down, about fifteen minutes.
3. Beat soup heavily until broken down to coarse puree, approximately half a minute. Adjust consistency with extra hot broth as required. Mix in lemon juice and sprinkle with salt and extra lemon juice to taste. Cover and keep warm.
4. Heat remaining 2 tablespoons oil in small frying pan on moderate heat until it starts to shimmer. Remove from the heat, mix in mint and paprika. Serve soup, drizzling individual portions with 1 teaspoon spiced oil and sprinkling with cilantro.

Tomato Soup with Eggplant Roast

Yield: 4 to 6 Servings

Ⓥ *This is a Vegetarian Recipe* Ⓥ

Eastern Mediterranean countries love to couple tomatoes with eggplant!

Ingredients:

- ¼ cup raisins
- ½ teaspoon ground cumin
- 1 (14.5-ounce) can diced tomatoes, drained
- 1 bay leaf
- 1 onion, chopped
- 1½ teaspoons ras el hanout
- 2 garlic cloves, minced
- 2 pounds eggplant, cut into ½-inch pieces
- 2 tablespoons minced fresh cilantro
- 2 tablespoons slivered almonds, toasted
- 2 teaspoons lemon juice
- 4 cups chicken or vegetable broth, plus extra as required
- 6 tablespoons extra-virgin olive oil, plus extra for serving
- Salt and pepper

Directions:

1. Place oven rack 4 inches from broiler element and heat broiler. Toss eggplant with 5 tablespoons oil, then spread in aluminum foil–lined rimmed baking sheet. Broil eggplant for about ten minutes. Stir eggplant and continue to broil until mahogany brown, 5 to 7 minutes. Measure out and reserve 2 cups eggplant.
2. Heat residual 1 tablespoon oil in a big saucepan on moderate heat until it starts to shimmer. Put in onion, ¾ teaspoon salt, and ¼ teaspoon pepper and cook till they become tender and lightly browned, 5 to 7 minutes. Mix in garlic, ras el hanout, and cumin and cook until aromatic, approximately half a minute. Mix in broth, tomatoes, raisins, bay leaf, and remaining eggplant and

bring to simmer. Decrease heat to low, cover, and simmer gently until eggplant is softened, approximately twenty minutes.

3. Discard bay leaf. Working in batches, process soup using a blender until smooth, approximately two minutes. Return soup to clean saucepan and mix in reserved eggplant. Heat soup gently over low heat until hot (do not boil) and adjust consistency with extra hot broth as required. Mix in lemon juice and sprinkle with salt and pepper to taste. Serve, sprinkling individual portions with almonds and cilantro and drizzling with extra oil.

Traditional Greek Avgolemono

Yield: 6 to 8 Servings

Ingredients:

- ½ cup long-grain white rice
- 1 bay leaf
- 1 scallion, sliced thin, or 3 tablespoons chopped fresh mint
- 1½ teaspoons salt
- 12 (4-inch) strips lemon zest plus ¼ cup juice (2 lemons)
- 2 large eggs plus 2 large yolks, room temperature
- 4 green cardamom pods, crushed, or 2 whole cloves
- 8 cups chicken broth

Directions:

1. Bring broth to boil in moderate-sized saucepan on high heat. Mix in rice, lemon zest, cardamom pods, bay leaf, and salt. Reduce to simmer and cook until rice becomes soft and broth is aromatic, 16 to 20 minutes.
2. Gently beat whole eggs, egg yolks, and lemon juice together in medium bowl until combined. Discard bay leaf, cardamom, and zest strips. Decrease heat to low. Whisking continuously, slowly ladle about 2 cups hot broth into egg mixture and beat until combined. Pour egg mixture back into saucepan and cook,

stirring continuously, until soup is slightly thickened and wisps of steam appear, approximately five minutes (do not simmer or boil). Sprinkle individual portions with scallion and serve instantly.

Turkish Tomato Grain Soup

Yield: 6 to 8 Servings

Ⓥ This is a Vegetarian Recipe Ⓥ

A Turkish tomato soup empowered by flavourful grains!

Ingredients:

- ⅛ teaspoon red pepper flakes
- ⅓ cup chopped fresh mint
- ½ cup dry white wine
- ½ teaspoon smoked paprika
- ¾ cup medium-grind bulgur, rinsed
- 1 (28-ounce) can diced fire-roasted tomatoes
- 1 onion, chopped
- 1 tablespoon tomato paste
- 1 teaspoon dried mint, crumbled
- 2 cups water
- 2 red bell peppers, stemmed, seeded, and chopped
- 2 tablespoons extra-virgin olive oil
- 3 garlic cloves, minced
- 4 cups chicken or vegetable broth
- Salt and pepper

Directions:

1. Heat oil in Dutch oven on moderate heat until it starts to shimmer. Put in onion, bell peppers, ¾ teaspoon salt, and ¼ teaspoon pepper and cook till they become tender and lightly browned, six to eight minutes. Mix in garlic, dried mint, smoked

paprika, and pepper flakes and cook until aromatic, approximately half a minute. Mix in tomato paste and cook for about sixty seconds.

2. Mix in wine, scraping up any browned bits, and simmer until reduced by half, about 1 minute. Put in tomatoes and their juice and cook, stirring intermittently, until tomatoes soften and begin to break apart, about 10 minutes.

3. Mix in broth, water, and bulgur and bring to simmer. Decrease heat to low, cover, and simmer gently until bulgur is tender, approximately twenty minutes. Drizzle with salt and pepper to taste. Serve, sprinkling individual portions with fresh mint.

Vegetable Broth Base

Yield: Approximately 1¾ cups base, or about 1¾ gallons broth

This recipe can be made quickly

This is a Vegetarian Recipe

A quick, easy, and flavourful vegetable broth.

Ingredients:

- ½ cup (½ ounce) fresh parsley leaves and thin stems
- ½ small celery root, peeled and cut into ½-inch pieces (¾ cup)
- 1 pound leeks, white and light green parts only, chopped and washed (2½ cups)
- 1½ tablespoons tomato paste
- 2 carrots, peeled and cut into ½-inch pieces (⅔ cup)
- 3 tablespoons dried minced onion
- 3 tablespoons kosher salt

Directions:

1. Process leeks, carrots, celery root, parsley, dried minced onion, and salt using a food processor, pausing to scrape down sides of the container often, until paste is as fine as possible, three to five

minutes. Put in tomato paste and process for 2 minutes, scraping down sides of the container every 30 seconds. Move mixture to airtight container and tap tightly on counter to eliminate air bubbles. Press small piece of parchment paper flush against surface of mixture and cover firmly. Freeze for maximum 6 months.

2. For each cup you wish to serve, stir 1 tablespoon fresh or frozen broth base into 1 cup boiling water. If particle-free broth is desired, allow broth to steep for about five minutes, then strain through fine-mesh strainer.

White Gazpacho

Yield: 6 to 8 Servings

Ⓥ This is a Vegetarian Recipe Ⓥ

A rich and elegant soup for when you want to impress!

Ingredients:

- ⅛ teaspoon almond extract
- ½ cup plus 2 teaspoons extra-virgin olive oil, plus extra for serving
- 1 garlic clove, peeled and smashed
- 2½ cups (8¾ ounces) plus ⅓ cup sliced blanched almonds
- 3 tablespoons sherry vinegar
- 4 cups water
- 6 ounces seedless green grapes, sliced thin (1 cup)
- 6 slices hearty white sandwich bread, crusts removed
- Pinch cayenne pepper
- Salt and pepper

Directions:

1. Mix bread and water in a container and let soak for about five minutes. Process 2½ cups almonds using a blender until finely ground, approximately half a minute, scraping down sides of

blender jar as required. Using your hands, remove bread from water, squeeze it lightly, and move to blender with almonds. Measure out 3 cups soaking water and set aside; move remaining soaking water to blender. Put in garlic, vinegar, ½ teaspoon salt, and cayenne to blender and process until mixture has consistency of cake batter, 30 to 45 seconds. With blender running, put in ½ cup oil in thin, steady stream, approximately half a minute. Put in reserved soaking water and process for about sixty seconds.

2. Season soup with salt and pepper to taste, then strain through fine-mesh strainer into a container, pressing on solids to extract as much liquid as possible; discard solids.
3. Move 1 tablespoon soup to different container and mix in almond extract. Return 1 teaspoon extract-soup mixture to soup; discard remaining mixture. Cover and put in the fridge to combine the flavours, minimum 4 hours or for maximum 24 hours.
4. Heat remaining 2 teaspoons oil in 8-inch frying pan on moderate to high heat until it starts to shimmer. Put in remaining ⅓ cup almonds and cook, stirring continuously, until golden brown, three to five minutes. Immediately move almonds to a container, mix in ¼ teaspoon salt, and allow to cool slightly.
5. Ladle soup into shallow bowls. Mound grapes in center of each bowl, drizzle with almonds, and drizzle with extra oil. Serve instantly.

Bonus: Salad and Salad Dressings

Salad Dressings

The dressing is the life of the salad.

Balsamic-Mustard Vinaigrette

Yield: ¼ cup

✗This recipe can be made quickly ✗

Ⓥ This is a Vegetarian Recipe Ⓥ

This is best for dressing assertive greens.

Ingredients:

- ⅛ teaspoon salt
- ½ teaspoon mayonnaise
- ½ teaspoon minced fresh thyme
- 1 tablespoon balsamic vinegar
- 1½ teaspoons minced shallot
- 2 teaspoons Dijon mustard
- 3 tablespoons extra-virgin olive oil
- Pinch pepper

Directions:

1. Beat vinegar, mustard, shallot, mayonnaise, thyme, salt, and pepper together in a container until smooth.
2. Whisking continuously, slowly drizzle in oil until completely blended. (Vinaigrette will keep safely in a fridge for maximum 2 weeks.)

Classic Vinaigrette

Yield: ¼ cup

✗This recipe can be made quickly ✗

Ⓥ This is a Vegetarian Recipe Ⓥ

This dressing works well with all types of greens.

Ingredients:

- ⅛ teaspoon salt
- ½ teaspoon Dijon mustard
- ½ teaspoon mayonnaise
- 1 tablespoon wine vinegar
- 1½ teaspoons minced shallot
- 3 tablespoons extra-virgin olive oil
- Pinch pepper

Directions:

1. Beat vinegar, shallot, mayonnaise, mustard, salt, and pepper together in a container until smooth.
2. Whisking continuously, slowly drizzle in oil until completely blended. (Vinaigrette will keep safely in a fridge for maximum 2 weeks.)

Herb Vinaigrette

Yield: ¼ cup

↗ *This recipe can be made quickly* ↗

Ⓥ *This is a Vegetarian Recipe* Ⓥ

Serve this vinaigrette immediately.

Ingredients:

- ⅛ teaspoon salt
- ½ teaspoon Dijon mustard
- ½ teaspoon mayonnaise
- ½ teaspoon minced fresh thyme, tarragon, marjoram, or oregano
- 1 tablespoon minced fresh parsley or chives
- 1 tablespoon wine vinegar

- 1½ teaspoons minced shallot
- 3 tablespoons extra-virgin olive oil
- Pinch pepper

Directions:

1. Beat vinegar, parsley, shallot, thyme, mayonnaise, mustard, salt, and pepper together in a container until smooth.
2. Whisking continuously, slowly drizzle in oil until completely blended.

Lemon Vinaigrette

Yield: ¼ cup

This recipe can be made quickly

Ⓥ This is a Vegetarian Recipe Ⓥ

This is best for dressing mild greens.

Ingredients:

- ⅛ teaspoon salt
- ¼ teaspoon grated lemon zest plus
- ½ teaspoon Dijon mustard
- ½ teaspoon mayonnaise
- 1 tablespoon juice
- 3 tablespoons extra-virgin olive oil
- Pinch pepper
- Pinch sugar

Directions:

1. Beat lemon zest and juice, mayonnaise, mustard, salt, pepper, and sugar together in a container until smooth.
2. Whisking continuously, slowly drizzle in oil until completely blended. (Vinaigrette will keep safely in a fridge for maximum 2 weeks.)

Tahini-Lemon Dressing

Yield: Approximately ½ cup

✎ This recipe can be made quickly ✎

Ⓥ This is a Vegetarian Recipe Ⓥ

Ingredients:

- ⅛ teaspoon pepper
- ¼ cup extra-virgin olive oil
- ½ teaspoon salt
- 1 garlic clove, minced
- 1 tablespoon water
- 2 tablespoons tahini
- 2½ tablespoons lemon juice

Directions:

1. Beat lemon juice, tahini, water, garlic, salt, and pepper together in a container until smooth.
2. Whisking continuously, slowly drizzle in oil until completely blended. (Dressing will keep safely in a fridge for maximum seven days.)

Walnut Vinaigrette

Yield: ¼ cup

✎ This recipe can be made quickly ✎

Ⓥ This is a Vegetarian Recipe Ⓥ

Ingredients:

- ⅛ teaspoon salt
- ½ teaspoon Dijon mustard
- ½ teaspoon mayonnaise
- 1 tablespoon wine vinegar
- 1½ tablespoons extra-virgin olive oil
- 1½ tablespoons roasted walnut oil
- 1½ teaspoons minced shallot
- Pinch pepper

Directions:

1. Beat vinegar, shallot, mayonnaise, mustard, salt, and pepper together in a container until smooth.
2. Whisking continuously, slowly drizzle in oils until completely blended. (Vinaigrette will keep safely in a fridge for maximum 2 weeks.)

Green Salads

Salads are a vital component of the Mediterranean diet. Enjoy these with a dressing of your choice!

Arugula Fennel Parmesan Salad

Yield: 4 to 6 Servings

This recipe can be made quickly

Ⓥ This is a Vegetarian Recipe Ⓥ

Ingredients:

- ¼ cup extra-virgin olive oil
- 1 large fennel bulb, stalks discarded, bulb halved, cored, and sliced thin
- 1 ounce Parmesan cheese, shaved

- 1 small garlic clove, minced
- 1 small shallot, minced
- 1 teaspoon Dijon mustard
- 1 teaspoon minced fresh thyme
- 1½ tablespoons lemon juice
- 6 ounces (6 cups) baby arugula
- Salt and pepper

Directions:

1. Gently toss arugula and fennel together in a big container. Beat lemon juice, shallot, mustard, thyme, garlic, ⅛ teaspoon salt, and pinch pepper together in a small-sized container.
2. Whisking continuously, slowly drizzle in oil. Sprinkle dressing over salad and gently toss to coat. Sprinkle with salt and pepper to taste. Serve, topping individual portions with Parmesan.

Arugula Mix Salad

Yield: 6 Servings

⚞ This recipe can be made quickly ⚟

Ingredients:

- ¼ cup extra-virgin olive oil
- ½ cup dried figs, stemmed and chopped
- ½ cup walnuts, toasted and chopped
- 1 small shallot, minced
- 1 tablespoon raspberry jam
- 2 ounces Parmesan cheese, shaved
- 2 ounces thinly sliced prosciutto, cut into ¼-inch-wide ribbons
- 3 tablespoons balsamic vinegar
- 8 ounces (8 cups) baby arugula
- Salt and pepper

Directions:

1. Heat 1 tablespoon oil in 10-inch non-stick frying pan on moderate heat. Put in prosciutto and cook, stirring frequently, until crisp, approximately seven minutes. Use a slotted spoon to move prosciutto to paper towel–lined plate; set aside.

2. Beat vinegar, jam, shallot, ¼ teaspoon salt, and ⅛ teaspoon pepper together in a big container. Mix in figs, cover, and microwave until steaming, about 1 minute. Whisking continuously, slowly drizzle in remaining 3 tablespoons oil. Allow to sit until figs are softened and vinaigrette has cooled to room temperature, about fifteen minutes.

3. Just before you serve, beat vinaigrette to re-emulsify. Put in arugula and gently toss to coat. Sprinkle with salt and pepper to taste. Serve, topping individual portions with prosciutto, walnuts, and Parmesan.

Arugula Sweet Salad

Yield: 6 Servings

✒ This recipe can be made quickly ✒

Ⓥ This is a Vegetarian Recipe Ⓥ

Honey can be substituted for the apricot jam.

Ingredients:

- ¼ small red onion, sliced thin
- ⅓ cup sliced almonds, toasted
- ½ cup dried apricots, chopped
- 1 ripe but firm pear, halved, cored, and sliced ¼ inch thick
- 1 small shallot, minced
- 1 tablespoon apricot jam
- 3 ounces goat cheese, crumbled (¾ cup)
- 3 tablespoons extra-virgin olive oil
- 3 tablespoons white wine vinegar
- 8 ounces (8 cups) baby arugula

- Salt and pepper

Directions:

1. Beat vinegar, jam, shallot, ¼ teaspoon salt, and ⅛ teaspoon pepper together in a big container. Put in apricots, cover, and microwave until steaming, about 1 minute. Whisking continuously, slowly drizzle in oil. Mix in onion and allow to sit until figs are softened and vinaigrette has cooled to room temperature, about fifteen minutes.
2. Just before you serve, beat vinaigrette to re-emulsify. Put in arugula and pear and gently toss to coat. Sprinkle with salt and pepper to taste. Serve, topping individual portions with almonds and goat cheese.

Asparagus Arugula Cannellini Salad

Yield: 4 to 6 Servings

✗ This recipe can be made quickly ✗

Ⓥ This is a Vegetarian Recipe Ⓥ

Ingredients:

- ½ red onion, sliced thin
- 1 (15-ounce) can cannellini beans, rinsed
- 1 pound asparagus, trimmed and cut on bias into 1-inch lengths
- 2 tablespoons plus 2 teaspoons balsamic vinegar
- 5 tablespoons extra-virgin olive oil
- 6 ounces (6 cups) baby arugula
- Salt and pepper

Directions:

1. Heat 2 tablespoons oil in 12-inch non-stick frying pan on high heat until just smoking. Put in onion and cook until lightly browned, about 1 minute. Put in asparagus, ¼ teaspoon salt, and

¼ teaspoon pepper and cook, stirring intermittently, until asparagus is browned and crisp-tender, about 4 minutes. Move to a container, mix in beans, and allow to cool slightly.

2. Beat vinegar, ¼ teaspoon salt, and ⅛ teaspoon pepper together in a small-sized container. Whisking continuously, slowly drizzle in remaining 3 tablespoons oil. Gently toss arugula with 2 tablespoons dressing until coated. Sprinkle with salt and pepper to taste. Divide arugula among plates. Toss asparagus mixture with remaining dressing, arrange over arugula, and serve.

Asparagus-Red Pepper-Spinach-Goat Cheese Salad

Yield: 4 to 6 Servings

✒ This recipe can be made quickly ✒

Ⓥ This is a Vegetarian Recipe Ⓥ

Ingredients:

- 1 garlic clove, minced
- 1 pound asparagus, trimmed and cut on bias into 1-inch lengths
- 1 red bell pepper, stemmed, seeded, and cut into 2-inch-long matchsticks
- 1 shallot, halved and sliced thin
- 1 tablespoon plus 1 teaspoon sherry vinegar
- 2 ounces goat cheese, crumbled (½ cup)
- 5 tablespoons extra-virgin olive oil
- 6 ounces (6 cups) baby spinach
- Salt and pepper

Directions:

1. Heat 1 tablespoon oil in 12-inch non-stick frying pan on high heat until just smoking. Put in bell pepper and cook until lightly browned, approximately two minutes. Put in asparagus, ¼

teaspoon salt, and ⅛ teaspoon pepper and cook, stirring intermittently, until asparagus is browned and almost tender, approximately two minutes. Mix in shallot and cook till they become tender and asparagus is crisp-tender, about 1 minute. Move to a container and allow to cool slightly.

2. Beat vinegar, garlic, ¼ teaspoon salt, and ⅛ teaspoon pepper together in a small-sized container. Whisking continuously, slowly drizzle in remaining ¼ cup oil. Gently toss spinach with 2 tablespoons dressing until coated. Sprinkle with salt and pepper to taste. Divide spinach among plates. Toss asparagus mixture with remaining dressing and arrange over spinach. Sprinkle with goat cheese and serve.

Bitter Greens Olive Feta Salad

Yield: 4 to 6 Servings

✦ This recipe can be made quickly ✦

Ⓥ This is a Vegetarian Recipe Ⓥ

Ingredients:

- ⅓ cup chopped fresh dill
- ⅓ cup pepperoncini, seeded and cut into ¼-inch-thick strips
- ½ cup pitted kalamata olives, halved
- 1 garlic clove, minced
- 1 head escarole (1 pound), trimmed and cut into 1-inch pieces
- 1 small head frisée (4 ounces), trimmed and torn into 1-inch pieces
- 2 ounces feta cheese, crumbled (½ cup)
- 2 tablespoons lemon juice
- 3 tablespoons extra-virgin olive oil
- Salt and pepper

Directions:

1. Gently toss escarole, frisée, olives, feta, and pepperoncini together in a big container. Beat dill, lemon juice, garlic, ¼ teaspoon salt, and ⅛ teaspoon pepper together in a small-sized container.
2. Whisking continuously, slowly drizzle in oil. Sprinkle dressing over salad and gently toss to coat. Serve.

Fiery Tuna-Olive Salad

Yield: 4 to 6 Servings

This recipe can be made quickly

Ingredients:

- ½ cup pimento-stuffed green olives, chopped
- 1 (15-ounce) can cannellini beans, rinsed
- 1 garlic clove, minced
- 1 tablespoon chopped fresh parsley
- 12 ounces cherry tomatoes, halved
- 2 (12-ounce) tuna steaks, 1 to 1¼ inches thick
- 3 tablespoons lemon juice
- 5 ounces (5 cups) baby arugula
- 6 tablespoons extra-virgin olive oil
- Salt and pepper

Directions:

1. Beat olives, lemon juice, parsley, and garlic together in a big container. Whisking continuously, slowly drizzle in 5 tablespoons oil. Sprinkle with salt and pepper to taste.
2. Pat tuna dry using paper towels and sprinkle with salt and pepper. Heat residual 1 tablespoon oil in 12-inch non-stick frying pan on moderate to high heat until just smoking. Cook tuna until thoroughly browned and translucent red at center when checked with tip of paring knife and registers 110 degrees (for rare),

approximately two minutes each side. Move to slicing board and slice into ½-inch-thick slices.

3. Beat dressing to re-emulsify, then drizzle 1 tablespoon dressing over tuna. Put in arugula, tomatoes, and beans to a container with remaining dressing and gently toss to combine. Sprinkle with salt and pepper to taste. Divide salad among plates and top with tuna. Serve.

Fundamental Green Salad

Yield: 4 Servings

✎ This recipe can be made quickly ✎

Ⓥ This is a Vegetarian Recipe Ⓥ

Ingredients:

- ½ garlic clove, peeled
- 8 ounces (8 cups) lettuce, torn into bite-size pieces if needed
- Extra-virgin olive oil
- Salt and pepper
- Vinegar

Directions:

1. Take a salad bowl and coat its inside with garlic. Put in lettuce. Cautiously sprinkle lettuce with a little oil. Slowly toss the contents of the bowl. Carry on drizzling with oil and toss gently until greens are mildly coated and barely starting to shine.
2. Drizzle with small amounts of vinegar, salt, and pepper to taste and toss gently to coat. Serve.

Green Artichoke Olive Salad

Yield: 4 to 6 Servings

⚡This recipe can be made quickly⚡

Ⓥ This is a Vegetarian Recipe Ⓥ

Ingredients:

- ⅓ cup fresh parsley leaves
- ⅓ cup pitted kalamata olives, halved
- 1 cup jarred whole baby artichoke hearts packed in water, quartered, rinsed, and patted dry
- 1 ounce Asiago cheese, shaved
- 1 romaine lettuce heart (6 ounces), cut into 1-inch pieces
- 1 small garlic clove, minced
- 2 tablespoons white wine vinegar or white balsamic vinegar
- 3 ounces (3 cups) baby arugula
- 3 tablespoons extra-virgin olive oil
- Salt and pepper

Directions:

1. Gently toss romaine, arugula, artichoke hearts, parsley, and olives together in a big container. Beat vinegar, garlic, ¼ teaspoon salt, and pinch pepper together in a small-sized container.
2. Whisking continuously, slowly drizzle in oil. Sprinkle vinaigrette over salad and gently toss to coat. Sprinkle with salt and pepper to taste. Serve, topping individual portions with Asiago.

Green Marcona Manchego Salad

Yield: 4 to 6 Servings

⚡This recipe can be made quickly⚡

(V) This is a Vegetarian Recipe (V)

Ingredients:

- ¼ cup extra-virgin olive oil
- ⅓ cup Marcona almonds, chopped coarse
- 1 shallot, minced
- 1 teaspoon Dijon mustard
- 2 ounces Manchego cheese, shaved
- 5 teaspoons sherry vinegar
- 6 ounces (6 cups) mesclun greens
- Salt and pepper

Directions:

1. Place mesclun in a big container. Beat vinegar, shallot, mustard, ¼ teaspoon salt, and ¼ teaspoon pepper together in a small-sized container. Whisking continuously, slowly drizzle in oil.
2. Sprinkle vinaigrette over mesclun and gently toss to coat. Sprinkle with salt and pepper to taste. Serve, topping individual portions with almonds and Manchego.

Kale-Sweet Potato Salad

Yield: 6 to 8 Servings

(V) This is a Vegetarian Recipe (V)

Ingredients:

SALAD

- ⅓ cup pecans, toasted and chopped
- ½ head radicchio (5 ounces), cored and sliced thin
- 1½ pounds sweet potatoes, peeled, cut into ½-inch pieces
- 12 ounces Tuscan kale, stemmed and sliced crosswise into ½-inch-wide strips (7 cups)
- 2 teaspoons extra-virgin olive oil

- Salt and pepper
- Shaved Parmesan cheese

VINAIGRETTE

- ¼ cup extra-virgin olive oil
- 1 small shallot, minced
- 1 tablespoon cider vinegar
- 1 tablespoon honey
- 1½ tablespoons pomegranate molasses
- 2 tablespoons water
- Salt and pepper

Directions:

1. **For the Salad:** Place the oven rack in the centre of the oven and pre-heat your oven to 400 degrees. Toss sweet potatoes with oil and sprinkle with salt and pepper. Arrange potatoes in one layer in rimmed baking sheet and roast until browned, 25 to 30 minutes, flipping potatoes halfway through roasting. Move to plate and allow to cool for 20 minutes. In the meantime, heavily squeeze and massage kale with hands until leaves are uniformly darkened and slightly wilted, about 1 minute.

2. **For the Vinaigrette**: Beat water, pomegranate molasses, shallot, honey, vinegar, ¼ teaspoon salt, and ¼ teaspoon pepper together in a big container. Whisking continuously, slowly drizzle in oil.

3. Put in potatoes, kale, and radicchio to vinaigrette and gently toss to coat. Sprinkle with salt and pepper to taste. Move to serving platter and drizzle with pecans and shaved Parmesan to taste. Serve.

Mâche-Cucumber-Mint Salad

Yield: **6 to 8 Servings**

✐ This recipe can be made quickly ✐

⓿ This is a Vegetarian Recipe ⓿

Ingredients:

- ¼ cup extra-virgin olive oil
- ⅓ cup pine nuts, toasted
- ½ cup chopped fresh mint
- 1 cucumber, sliced thin
- 1 garlic clove, minced
- 1 tablespoon capers, rinsed and minced
- 1 tablespoon lemon juice
- 1 tablespoon minced fresh parsley
- 1 teaspoon minced fresh thyme
- 12 ounces (12 cups) mâche
- Salt and pepper

Directions:

1. Gently toss mâche, cucumber, mint, and pine nuts together in a big container. Beat lemon juice, parsley, capers, thyme, garlic, ¼ teaspoon salt, and ¼ teaspoon pepper together in a small-sized container.
2. Whisking continuously, slowly drizzle in oil. Sprinkle dressing over salad and gently toss to coat. Sprinkle with salt and pepper to taste. Serve.

Salade Niçoise

Yield: 6 Servings

Ingredients:

DRESSING

- ¼ cup lemon juice (2 lemons)
- ¼ teaspoon pepper
- ½ cup extra-virgin olive oil
- ½ teaspoon salt

- 1 shallot, minced
- 1 teaspoon Dijon mustard
- 2 tablespoons minced fresh basil
- 2 teaspoons minced fresh oregano
- 2 teaspoons minced fresh thyme

SALAD

- ¼ cup pitted niçoise olives
- 1 small red onion, sliced thin
- 10–12 anchovy fillets, rinsed (optional)
- 1¼ pounds small red potatoes, unpeeled, quartered
- 2 (5-ounce) cans solid white tuna in water, drained and flaked
- 2 heads Boston lettuce or Bibb lettuce (1 pound), torn into bite-size pieces
- 2 tablespoons capers, rinsed (optional)
- 2 tablespoons dry vermouth
- 3 hard-cooked large eggs, peeled and quartered
- 3 small tomatoes, cored and cut into ½-inch-thick wedges
- 8 ounces green beans, trimmed and halved
- Salt and pepper

Directions:

1. **FOR THE DRESSING**: Beat lemon juice, shallot, basil, thyme, oregano, mustard, salt, and pepper together in a small-sized container. Whisking continuously, slowly drizzle in oil.
2. **FOR THE SALAD**: Place potatoes in a big saucepan, put in water to cover by 1 inch, and bring to boil on high heat. Put in 1 tablespoon salt, reduce to simmer, and cook until potatoes are soft and paring knife can be slipped in and out of potatoes with little resistance, 5 to 8 minutes. With slotted spoon, gently move potatoes to a container (do not discard water). Toss warm potatoes with ¼ cup vinaigrette and vermouth. Sprinkle with salt and pepper to taste; set aside.
3. As potatoes cook, mildly toss lettuce with ¼ cup vinaigrette in a container until coated. Arrange bed of lettuce on very large, flat serving platter. Place tuna in now-empty bowl and break up

using a fork. Put in ¼ cup vinaigrette and stir to combine. Mound tuna in center of lettuce. In now-empty bowl, toss tomatoes and red onion with 2 tablespoons vinaigrette and sprinkle with salt and pepper to taste. Arrange tomato-onion mixture in mound at edge of lettuce bed. Arrange rest of the potatoes in separate mound at edge of lettuce bed.

4. Return water to boil and put in 1 tablespoon salt and green beans. Cook until crisp-tender, 3 to 5 minutes. In the meantime, fill big container halfway with ice and water. Drain green beans, move to ice water, and allow to sit until just cool, approximately half a minute. Move beans to triple layer of paper towels and dry well. In now-empty bowl, toss green beans with remaining 2 tablespoons vinaigrette and sprinkle with salt and pepper to taste. Arrange in separate mound at edge of lettuce bed.

5. Place eggs, olives, and anchovies, if using, in separate mounds at edge of lettuce bed. Sprinkle the whole salad with capers, if using. Serve.

Spinach-Feta-Pistachio Salad

Yield: 6 Servings

✀ This recipe can be made quickly ✀

Ⓥ This is a Vegetarian Recipe Ⓥ

Ingredients:

- 1 (2-inch) strip lemon zest plus 1½ tablespoons juice
- 1 shallot, minced
- 10 ounces curly-leaf spinach, stemmed and torn into bite-size pieces
- 1½ ounces feta cheese, crumbled (⅓ cup)
- 2 teaspoons sugar
- 3 tablespoons chopped toasted pistachios
- 3 tablespoons extra-virgin olive oil
- 6 radishes, trimmed and sliced thin

- Salt and pepper

Directions:

1. Place feta on plate and freeze until mildly stiff, about fifteen minutes.
2. Cook oil, lemon zest, shallot, and sugar in Dutch oven over moderate to low heat until shallot is softened, approximately five minutes. Remove from the heat, discard zest and mix in lemon juice. Put in spinach, cover, and let steam off heat until it just begins to wilt, approximately half a minute.
3. Move spinach mixture and liquid left in pot to big container. Put in radishes, pistachios, and chilled feta and toss to combine. Sprinkle with salt and pepper to taste. Serve.

Tangy Salad

Yield: 4 to 6 Servings

This recipe can be made quickly

This is a Vegetarian Recipe

Ingredients:

- ½ cup smoked almonds, chopped coarse
- ⅔ cup chopped pitted dates
- 1 small head radicchio (6 ounces), cored and sliced thin
- 1 small shallot, minced
- 1 teaspoon Dijon mustard
- 1 teaspoon sugar
- 2 red grapefruits
- 3 oranges
- 3 tablespoons extra-virgin olive oil
- Salt and pepper

Directions:

1. Cut away peel and pith from grapefruits and oranges. Cut each fruit in half from pole to pole, then slice crosswise ¼ inch thick. Move to a container, toss with sugar and ½ teaspoon salt, and allow to sit for about fifteen minutes.
2. Drain fruit in fine-mesh strainer set over bowl, reserving 2 tablespoons juice. Arrange fruit on serving platter and drizzle with oil. Beat reserved juice, shallot, and mustard together in medium bowl. Put in radicchio, ⅓ cup dates, and ¼ cup almonds and gently toss to coat. Sprinkle with salt and pepper to taste. Arrange radicchio mixture over fruit, leaving 1-inch border of fruit around edges. Sprinkle with remaining ⅓ cup dates and remaining ¼ cup almonds. Serve.

Tri-Balsamic Salad

Yield: 4 to 6 Servings

✦ This recipe can be made quickly ✦

Ⓥ *This is a Vegetarian Recipe* Ⓥ

Ingredients:

- 1 head Belgian endive (4 ounces), cut into 2-inch pieces
- 1 small head radicchio (6 ounces), cored and cut into 1-inch pieces
- 1 tablespoon balsamic vinegar
- 1 teaspoon red wine vinegar
- 3 ounces (3 cups) baby arugula
- 3 tablespoons extra-virgin olive oil
- Salt and pepper

Directions:

1. Gently toss radicchio, endive, and arugula together in a big container. Beat balsamic vinegar, red wine vinegar, ⅛ teaspoon salt, and pinch pepper together in a small-sized container.

2. Whisking continuously, slowly drizzle in oil. Drizzle vinaigrette over salad and gently toss to coat. Drizzle with salt and pepper to taste. Serve.

Vegetable Salads

Algerian Mix Salad

Yield: 4 to 6 Servings

✗This recipe can be made quickly ✗

Ⓥ This is a Vegetarian Recipe Ⓥ

Ingredients:

- ¼ cup coarsely chopped fresh mint
- ¼ cup extra-virgin olive oil
- ½ cup pitted oil-cured black olives, quartered
- 2 fennel bulbs, stalks discarded, bulbs halved, cored, and sliced thin
- 2 tablespoons lemon juice
- 4 blood oranges
- Salt and pepper

Directions:

1. Cut away peel and pith from oranges. Quarter oranges, then slice crosswise into ¼-inch-thick pieces. Mix oranges, fennel, olives, and mint in a big container.
2. Beat lemon juice, ¼ teaspoon salt, and ⅛ teaspoon pepper together in a small-sized container. Whisking continuously, slowly drizzle in oil. Sprinkle dressing over salad and gently toss to coat. Sprinkle with salt and pepper to taste. Serve.

Asparagus Mix Salad

Yield: 4 to 6 Servings

✄ *This recipe can be made quickly* ✄

Ⓥ *This is a Vegetarian Recipe* Ⓥ

Ingredients:

PESTO

- ¼ cup fresh basil leaves
- ¼ cup grated Pecorino Romano cheese
- ½ cup extra-virgin olive oil
- 1 garlic clove, minced
- 1 teaspoon grated lemon zest plus 2 teaspoons juice
- 2 cups fresh mint leaves
- Salt and pepper

SALAD

- ¾ cup hazelnuts, toasted, skinned, and chopped
- 2 oranges
- 2 pounds asparagus, trimmed
- 4 ounces feta cheese, crumbled (1 cup)
- Salt and pepper

Directions:

1. **For the Pesto:** Process mint, basil, Pecorino, lemon zest and juice, garlic, and ¾ teaspoon salt using a food processor until finely chopped, approximately half a minute, scraping down sides of the container as required. Move to big container. Mix in oil and sprinkle with salt and pepper to taste.
2. **For the Salad:** Chop asparagus tips from stalks into ¾-inch-long pieces. Cut asparagus stalks ⅛ inch thick on bias into approximate 2-inch lengths. Cut away the peel and pith from oranges. Holding fruit over bowl, use paring knife to cut between membranes to release segments. Put in asparagus tips and

stalks, orange segments, feta, and hazelnuts to pesto and toss to combine. Sprinkle with salt and pepper to taste. Serve.

Brussels Pecorino Pine Salad

Yield: 4 to 6 Servings

This recipe can be made quickly

Ⓥ This is a Vegetarian Recipe Ⓥ

Ingredients:

- ¼ cup extra-virgin olive oil
- ¼ cup pine nuts, toasted
- 1 garlic clove, minced
- 1 pound Brussels sprouts, trimmed, halved, and sliced very thin
- 1 small shallot, minced
- 1 tablespoon Dijon mustard
- 2 ounces Pecorino Romano cheese, shredded (⅔ cup)
- 2 tablespoons lemon juice
- Salt and pepper

Directions:

1. Beat lemon juice, mustard, shallot, garlic, and ½ teaspoon salt together in a big container. Whisking continuously, slowly drizzle in oil. Put in Brussels sprouts, toss to coat, and allow to sit for minimum half an hour or maximum 2 hours.
2. Mix in Pecorino and pine nuts. Sprinkle with salt and pepper to taste. Serve.

Cauliflower Chermoula Salad

Yield: 4 to 6 Servings

Ingredients:

SALAD

- ½ cup raisins
- ½ red onion, sliced ¼ inch thick
- 1 cup shredded carrot
- 1 head cauliflower (2 pounds), cored and cut into 2-inch florets
- 2 tablespoons chopped fresh cilantro
- 2 tablespoons extra-virgin olive oil
- 2 tablespoons sliced almonds, toasted
- Salt and pepper

CHERMOULA

- ⅛ teaspoon cayenne pepper
- ¼ cup extra-virgin olive oil
- ¼ teaspoon salt
- ½ teaspoon ground cumin
- ½ teaspoon paprika
- ¾ cup fresh cilantro leaves
- 2 tablespoons lemon juice
- 4 garlic cloves, minced

Directions:

1. **For the Salad:** Place oven rack to lowest position and pre-heat your oven to 475 degrees. Toss cauliflower with oil and sprinkle with salt and pepper. Arrange cauliflower in one layer in parchment paper–lined rimmed baking sheet. Cover tightly with aluminium foil and roast till they become tender, 5 to 7 minutes. Remove foil and spread onion evenly in sheet. Roast until vegetables are tender, cauliflower becomes deeply golden brown, and onion slices are charred at edges, 10 to fifteen minutes, stirring halfway through roasting. Allow it to cool slightly, approximately five minutes.

2. **For the Chermoula:** Process all ingredients using a food processor until smooth, about 1 minute, scraping down sides of the container as required. Move to big container.

3. Gently toss cauliflower-onion mixture, carrot, raisins, and cilantro with chermoula until coated. Move to serving platter and drizzle with almonds. Serve warm or at room temperature.

Cherry Tomato Mix Salad

Yield: 4 to 6 Servings

Ⓥ *This is a Vegetarian Recipe* Ⓥ

Ingredients:

- ½ cup pitted kalamata olives, chopped
- ½ teaspoon sugar
- 1 shallot, minced
- 1 small cucumber, peeled, halved along the length, seeded, and cut into ½-inch pieces
- 1 tablespoon red wine vinegar
- 1½ pounds cherry tomatoes, quartered
- 2 garlic cloves, minced
- 2 tablespoons extra-virgin olive oil
- 2 teaspoons minced fresh oregano
- 3 tablespoons chopped fresh parsley
- 4 ounces feta cheese, crumbled (1 cup)
- Salt and pepper

Directions:

1. Toss tomatoes with sugar and ¼ teaspoon salt in a container and allow to sit for 30 minutes. Move tomatoes to salad spinner and spin until seeds and excess liquid have been removed, 45 to 60 seconds, stopping to redistribute tomatoes several times during spinning. Put in tomatoes, cucumber, olives, feta, and parsley to big container; set aside.

2. Strain ½ cup tomato liquid through fine-mesh strainer into liquid measuring cup; discard remaining liquid. Bring tomato liquid, shallot, vinegar, garlic, and oregano to simmer in small saucepan on moderate heat and cook until reduced to 3 tablespoons, six to eight minutes. Move to small-sized container and allow to cool to room temperature, approximately five minutes. Whisking continuously, slowly drizzle in oil. Sprinkle dressing over salad and gently toss to coat. Sprinkle with salt and pepper to taste. Serve.

Classic Greek Salad

Yield: 6 to 8 Servings

This recipe can be made quickly

Ⓥ *This is a Vegetarian Recipe* Ⓥ

Ingredients:

- ¼ cup chopped fresh mint
- ¼ cup chopped fresh parsley
- ½ cup pitted kalamata olives, quartered
- ½ red onion, sliced thin
- 1 cup jarred roasted red peppers, rinsed, patted dry, and cut into ½-inch strips
- 1 garlic clove, minced
- 1 teaspoon lemon juice
- 1½ tablespoons red wine vinegar
- 2 cucumbers, peeled, halved along the length, seeded, and sliced thin
- 2 teaspoons minced fresh oregano
- 5 ounces feta cheese, crumbled (1¼ cups)
- 6 large ripe tomatoes, cored, seeded, and cut into ½-inch-thick wedges
- 6 tablespoons extra-virgin olive oil

- Salt and pepper

Directions:

1. Beat oil, vinegar, oregano, lemon juice, garlic, ½ teaspoon salt, and ⅛ teaspoon pepper together in a big container. Put in cucumbers and onion, toss to coat, and allow to sit for 20 minutes.
2. Put in tomatoes, red peppers, olives, parsley, and mint to a container with cucumber-onion mixture and toss to combine. Sprinkle with salt and pepper to taste. Move salad to wide, shallow serving bowl or platter and drizzle with feta. Serve instantly.

Crunchy Mushroom Salad

Yield: 6 Servings

✐ This recipe can be made quickly ✐

Ⓥ This is a Vegetarian Recipe Ⓥ

Ingredients:

- ¼ cup extra-virgin olive oil
- ½ cup fresh parsley leaves
- 1 shallot, halved and sliced thin
- 1½ tablespoons lemon juice
- 2 ounces Parmesan cheese, shaved
- 2 tablespoons chopped fresh tarragon
- 4 celery ribs, sliced thin, plus ½ cup celery leaves
- 8 ounces cremini mushrooms, trimmed and sliced thin
- Salt and pepper

Directions:

1. Beat oil, lemon juice, and ¼ teaspoon salt together in a big container. Put in mushrooms and shallot, toss to coat, and allow to sit for about ten minutes.
2. Put in sliced celery and leaves, Parmesan, parsley, and tarragon to mushroom-shallot mixture and toss to combine. Sprinkle with salt and pepper to taste. Serve.

Cucumber Sesame-Lemon Salad

Yield: 4 Servings

Ⓥ *This is a Vegetarian Recipe* Ⓥ

Ingredients:

- ⅛ teaspoon red pepper flakes, plus extra for seasoning
- ¼ cup rice vinegar
- 1 tablespoon lemon juice
- 1 tablespoon sesame seeds, toasted
- 2 tablespoons toasted sesame oil
- 2 teaspoons sugar
- 3 cucumbers, peeled, halved along the length, seeded, and sliced ¼ inch thick
- Salt and pepper

Directions:

1. Toss cucumbers with 1 tablespoon salt using a colander set over big container. Weight cucumbers with 1 gallon-size zipper-lock bag filled with water; drain for 1 to three hours. Wash and pat dry.
2. Beat vinegar, oil, lemon juice, sesame seeds, sugar, and pepper flakes together in a big container. Put in cucumbers and toss to coat. Sprinkle with salt and pepper to taste. Serve at room temperature or chilled.

Cut Up Salad

Yield: 4 Servings

Ⓥ This is a Vegetarian Recipe Ⓥ

Ingredients:

- ½ cup chopped fresh parsley
- ½ cup pitted kalamata olives, chopped
- ½ small red onion, chopped fine
- 1 (15-ounce) can chickpeas, rinsed
- 1 cucumber, peeled, halved along the length, seeded, and cut into ½-inch pieces
- 1 garlic clove, minced
- 1 romaine lettuce heart (6 ounces), cut into ½-inch pieces
- 10 ounces grape tomatoes, quartered
- 3 tablespoons extra-virgin olive oil
- 3 tablespoons red wine vinegar
- 4 ounces feta cheese, crumbled (1 cup)
- Salt and pepper

Directions:

1. Toss cucumber and tomatoes with 1 teaspoon salt and allow to drain using a colander for about fifteen minutes.
2. Beat vinegar and garlic together in a big container. Whisking continuously, slowly drizzle in oil. Put in cucumber-tomato mixture, chickpeas, olives, onion, and parsley and toss to coat. Allow to sit for minimum 5 minutes or maximum 20 minutes.
3. Put in lettuce and feta and gently toss to combine. Sprinkle with salt and pepper to taste. Serve.

Fattoush

Yield: 4 to 6 Servings

Ⓥ This is a Vegetarian Recipe Ⓥ

Ingredients:

- ¼ teaspoon minced garlic
- ½ cup chopped fresh cilantro
- ½ cup chopped fresh mint
- 1 cup arugula, chopped coarse
- 1 English cucumber, peeled and sliced ⅛ inch thick
- 1 pound ripe tomatoes, cored and cut into ¾-inch pieces
- 2 (8-inch) pita breads
- 3 tablespoons lemon juice
- 4 scallions, sliced thin
- 4 teaspoons ground sumac, plus extra for sprinkling
- 7 tablespoons extra-virgin olive oil
- Salt and pepper

Directions:

1. Place the oven rack in the centre of the oven and pre-heat your oven to 375 degrees. Using kitchen shears, slice around perimeter of each pita and divide into 2 thin rounds. Cut each round in half. Place pitas smooth side down on wire rack set in rimmed baking sheet. Brush 3 tablespoons oil on surface of pitas. (Pitas do not need to be uniformly coated. Oil will spread during baking.) Sprinkle with salt and pepper. Bake until pitas are crisp and pale golden brown, 10 to 14 minutes. Allow it to cool to room temperature.
2. Beat lemon juice, sumac, garlic, and ¼ teaspoon salt together in a small-sized container and allow to sit for about ten minutes. Whisking continuously, slowly drizzle in remaining ¼ cup oil.
3. Break pitas into ½-inch pieces and place in a big container. Put in tomatoes, cucumber, arugula, cilantro, mint, and scallions. Sprinkle dressing over salad and gently toss to coat. Sprinkle with

salt and pepper to taste. Serve, sprinkling individual portions with extra sumac.

French Potato Dijon Herb Salad

Yield: 4 to 6 Servings

Ⓥ This is a Vegetarian Recipe Ⓥ

Ingredients:

- ¼ cup extra-virgin olive oil
- ½ teaspoon pepper
- 1 garlic clove, peeled and threaded on skewer
- 1 small shallot, minced
- 1 tablespoon minced fresh chervil
- 1 tablespoon minced fresh chives
- 1 tablespoon minced fresh parsley
- 1 teaspoon minced fresh tarragon
- 1½ tablespoons white wine vinegar or Champagne vinegar
- 2 pounds small red potatoes, unpeeled, sliced ¼ inch thick
- 2 tablespoons salt
- 2 teaspoons Dijon mustard

Directions:

1. Place potatoes in a big saucepan, put in water to cover by 1 inch, and bring to boil on high heat. Put in salt, decrease the heat to simmer, and cook until potatoes are soft and paring knife can be slipped in and out of potatoes with little resistance, about 6 minutes.
2. While potatoes are cooking, lower skewered garlic into simmering water and blanch for 45 seconds. Run garlic under cold running water, then remove from skewer and mince.
3. Reserve ¼ cup cooking water, then drain potatoes and lay out on tight one layer in rimmed baking sheet. Beat oil, minced garlic, vinegar, mustard, pepper, and reserved potato cooking water

together in a container, then drizzle over potatoes. Let potatoes sit until flavours blend, about 10 minutes. (Potatoes will keep safely in a fridge for maximum 8 hours; return to room temperature before you serve.)

4. Move potatoes to big container. Mix shallot and herbs in a small-sized container, then drizzle over potatoes and gently toss to coat using rubber spatula. Serve.

Green Bean Cilantro Salad

Yield: 6 to 8 Servings

✿ This recipe can be made quickly ✿

Ⓥ This is a Vegetarian Recipe Ⓥ

Ingredients:

- ¼ cup walnuts
- ½ cup extra-virgin olive oil
- 1 scallion, sliced thin
- 2 garlic cloves, unpeeled
- 2 pounds green beans, trimmed
- 2½ cups fresh cilantro leaves and stems, tough stem ends trimmed (about 2 bunches)
- 4 teaspoons lemon juice
- Salt and pepper

Directions:

1. Cook walnuts and garlic in 8-inch frying pan on moderate heat, stirring frequently, until toasted and aromatic, 5 to 7 minutes; move to a container. Let garlic cool slightly, then peel and approximately chop.
2. Process walnuts, garlic, cilantro, oil, lemon juice, scallion, ½ teaspoon salt, and ⅛ teaspoon pepper using a food processor

until smooth, about 1 minute, scraping down sides of the container as required; move to big container.

3. Bring 4 quarts water to boil in large pot on high heat. In the meantime, fill big container halfway with ice and water. Put in 1 tablespoon salt and green beans to boiling water and cook until crisp-tender, 3 to 5 minutes. Drain green beans, move to ice water, and allow to sit until chilled, approximately two minutes. Move green beans to a container with cilantro sauce and gently toss until coated. Sprinkle with salt and pepper to taste. Serve. (Salad will keep safely in a fridge for maximum 4 hours.)

Halloumi-Veg Salad

Yield: 4 to 6 Servings

This recipe can be made quickly

(V) This is a Vegetarian Recipe (V)

Ingredients:

- ¼ cup extra-virgin olive oil
- ½ teaspoon grated lemon zest plus 3 tablespoons juice
- 1 (8-ounce) block halloumi cheese, sliced into ½-inch-thick slabs
- 1 garlic clove, minced
- 1 head radicchio (10 ounces), quartered
- 1 pound eggplant, sliced into ½-inch-thick rounds
- 1 tablespoon minced fresh thyme
- 1 zucchini, halved along the length
- 3 tablespoons honey
- Salt and pepper

Directions:

1. Beat honey, thyme, lemon zest and juice, garlic, ⅛ teaspoon salt, and ⅛ teaspoon pepper together in a big container; set aside.

Brush eggplant, radicchio, zucchini, and halloumi with 2 tablespoons oil and sprinkle with salt and pepper.

2. **FOR A CHARCOAL GRILL:** Open bottom vent fully. Light large chimney starter half filled with charcoal briquettes (3 quarts). When top coals are partially covered with ash, pour uniformly over grill. Set cooking grate in place, cover, and open lid vent fully. Heat grill until hot, approximately five minutes.

3. **FOR A GAS GRILL:** Turn all burners to high, cover, and heat grill until hot, about fifteen minutes. Turn all burners to medium.

4. Clean cooking grate, then repetitively brush grate with thoroughly oiled paper towels until grate is black and glossy, 5 to 10 times. Place vegetables and cheese on grill. Cook (covered if using gas), flipping as required, until radicchio becomes tender and mildly charred, 3 to 5 minutes, and remaining vegetables and cheese are softened and mildly charred, about 10 minutes. Move vegetables and cheese to slicing board as they finish cooking, allow to cool slightly, then cut into 1-inch pieces.

5. Whisking continuously, slowly drizzle remaining 2 tablespoons oil into honey mixture. Put in vegetables and cheese and gently toss to coat. Sprinkle with salt and pepper to taste. Serve.

Italian Panzanella Mix Salad

Yield: 6 Servings

Ⓥ This is a Vegetarian Recipe Ⓥ

Ingredients:

- 1 (15-ounce) can cannellini beans, rinsed
- 1 small red onion, halved and sliced thin
- 1½ pounds ripe tomatoes, cored and chopped, seeds and juice reserved
- 12 ounces rustic Italian bread, cut into 1-inch pieces (4 cups)
- 2 ounces Parmesan cheese, shaved
- 2 tablespoons minced fresh oregano

- 3 ounces (3 cups) baby arugula
- 3 tablespoons chopped fresh basil
- 3 tablespoons red wine vinegar
- 5 tablespoons extra-virgin olive oil
- Salt and pepper

Directions:

1. Place the oven rack in the centre of the oven and pre-heat your oven to 350 degrees. Toss bread pieces with 1 tablespoon oil and sprinkle with salt and pepper. Arrange bread in one layer in rimmed baking sheet and bake, stirring intermittently, until light golden brown, fifteen to twenty minutes. Allow it to cool to room temperature.
2. Beat vinegar and ¼ teaspoon salt together in a big container. Whisking continuously, slowly drizzle in remaining ¼ cup oil. Put in tomatoes with their seeds and juice, beans, onion, 1½ tablespoons basil, and 1 tablespoon oregano, toss to coat, and allow to sit for 20 minutes.
3. Put in cooled croutons, arugula, remaining 1½ tablespoons basil, and remaining 1 tablespoon oregano and gently toss to combine. Sprinkle with salt and pepper to taste. Move salad to serving platter and drizzle with Parmesan. Serve.

Mackerel-Fennel-Apple Salad

Yield: 4 to 6 Servings

Ingredients:

- ¼ cup extra-virgin olive oil
- 1 fennel bulb, stalks discarded, bulb halved, cored, and sliced thin
- 1 small shallot, minced
- 1 tablespoon whole-grain mustard
- 2 Granny Smith apples, peeled, cored, and cut into 3-inch-long matchsticks

- 2 teaspoons minced fresh tarragon
- 3 tablespoons lemon juice
- 5 ounces (5 cups) watercress
- 6 ounces smoked mackerel, skin and pin bones removed, flaked
- Salt and pepper

Directions:

1. Beat lemon juice, mustard, shallot, 1 teaspoon tarragon, ½ teaspoon salt, and ¼ teaspoon pepper together in a big container. Whisking continuously, slowly drizzle in oil. Put in watercress, apples, and fennel and gently toss to coat. Sprinkle with salt and pepper to taste.
2. Divide salad among plates and top with flaked mackerel. Sprinkle any remaining dressing over mackerel and drizzle with remaining 1 teaspoon tarragon. Serve instantly.

Moroccan Carrot Salad

Yield: 4 to 6 Servings

✗ This recipe can be made quickly ✗

Ⓥ *This is a Vegetarian Recipe* Ⓥ

Ingredients:

- ⅛ teaspoon cayenne pepper
- ⅛ teaspoon ground cinnamon
- ¾ teaspoon ground cumin
- 1 pound carrots, peeled and shredded
- 1 tablespoon lemon juice
- 1 teaspoon honey
- 2 oranges
- 3 tablespoons extra-virgin olive oil
- 3 tablespoons minced fresh cilantro
- Salt and pepper

Directions:

1. Cut away peel and pith from oranges. Holding fruit over bowl, use paring knife to slice between membranes to release segments. Cut segments in half crosswise and allow to drain in fine-mesh strainer set over big container, reserving juice.
2. Beat lemon juice, honey, cumin, cayenne, cinnamon, and ½ teaspoon salt into reserved orange juice. Put in drained oranges and carrots and gently toss to coat. Allow to sit until liquid starts to pool in bottom of bowl, 3 to 5 minutes.
3. Drain salad in fine-mesh strainer and return to now-empty bowl. Mix in cilantro and oil and sprinkle with salt and pepper to taste. Serve.

Radish-Fava Salad

Yield: 4 to 6 Servings

This recipe can be made quickly

This is a Vegetarian Recipe

Ingredients:

- ¼ cup chopped fresh basil
- ¼ cup extra-virgin olive oil
- ¼ teaspoon ground coriander
- ¼ teaspoon pepper
- ½ teaspoon salt
- 10 radishes, trimmed, halved, and sliced thin
- 1½ ounces (1½ cups) pea shoots
- 2 garlic cloves, minced
- 3 pounds fava beans, shelled (3 cups)
- 3 tablespoons lemon juice

Directions:

1. Bring 4 quarts water to boil in large pot on high heat. In the meantime, fill big container halfway with ice and water. Put in fava beans to boiling water and cook for about sixty seconds. Drain fava beans, move to ice water, and allow to sit until chilled, approximately two minutes. Move fava beans to triple layer of paper towels and dry well. Use a pairing knife to make small cut along edge of each bean through waxy sheath, then gently squeeze sheath to release bean; discard sheath.

2. Beat lemon juice, garlic, salt, pepper, and coriander together in a big container. Whisking continuously, slowly drizzle in oil. Put in fava beans, radishes, pea shoots, and basil and gently toss to coat. Serve instantly.

Roasted Beet-Carrot Salad with

Yield: 4 to 6 Servings

Ⓥ *This is a Vegetarian Recipe* Ⓥ

Ingredients:

- ½ cup shelled pistachios, toasted and chopped
- ½ teaspoon ground cumin
- 1 pound beets, trimmed
- 1 pound carrots, peeled and sliced on bias ¼ inch thick
- 1 small shallot, minced
- 1 tablespoon grated lemon zest plus 3 tablespoons juice
- 1 teaspoon honey
- 2 tablespoons minced fresh parsley
- 2½ tablespoons extra-virgin olive oil
- Salt and pepper

Directions:

1. Adjust oven racks to middle and lowest positions. Place rimmed baking sheet on lower rack and pre-heat your oven to 450 degrees.

2. Wrap each beet individually in aluminium foil and place in second rimmed baking sheet. Toss carrots with 1 tablespoon oil, ½ teaspoon salt, and ½ teaspoon pepper.
3. Quickly, arrange carrots in one layer in hot baking sheet and place baking sheet with beets on middle rack. Roast until carrots are soft and thoroughly browned on 1 side, 20 minutes to half an hour, and skewer can be inserted easily into the center of the beets with aluminium foil removed 35 to 45 minutes.
4. Cautiously open foil packets and allow beets to sit until cool enough to handle. Cautiously rub off beet skins using paper towel. Slice beets into ½-inch-thick wedges, and, if large, cut in half crosswise.
5. Beat lemon juice, shallot, honey, cumin, ¼ teaspoon salt, and ⅛ teaspoon pepper together in a big container. Whisking continuously, slowly drizzle in remaining 1½ tablespoons oil. Put in beets and carrots, toss to coat, and allow to cool to room temperature, approximately twenty minutes.
6. Put in pistachios, parsley, and lemon zest to a container with beets and carrots and toss to coat. Sprinkle with salt and pepper to taste. Serve.

Scorched Beet Almond Salad

Yield: 4 to 6 Servings

Ⓥ *This is a Vegetarian Recipe* Ⓥ

Ingredients:

- 2 blood oranges
- 2 ounces (2 cups) baby arugula
- 2 ounces ricotta salata cheese, shaved
- 2 pounds beets, trimmed
- 2 tablespoons extra-virgin olive oil
- 2 tablespoons sliced almonds, toasted
- 4 teaspoons sherry vinegar

- Salt and pepper

Directions:

1. Place the oven rack in the centre of the oven and pre-heat your oven to 400 degrees. Wrap each beet individually in aluminium foil and place in rimmed baking sheet. Roast beets until it is easy to skewer the centre of beets with foil removed, forty minutes to one hour.
2. Cautiously open foil packets and allow beets to sit until cool enough to handle. Cautiously rub off beet skins using a paper towel. Slice beets into ½-inch-thick wedges, and, if large, cut in half crosswise.
3. Beat vinegar, ¼ teaspoon salt, and ¼ teaspoon pepper together in a big container. Whisking continuously, slowly drizzle in oil. Put in beets, toss to coat, and allow to cool to room temperature, approximately twenty minutes.
4. Cut away peel and pith from oranges. Quarter oranges, then slice crosswise into ½-inch-thick pieces. Put in oranges and arugula to a container with beets and gently toss to coat. Sprinkle with salt and pepper to taste. Move to serving platter and drizzle with ricotta salata and almonds. Serve.

Sweet Nut Winter Squash Salad

Yield: 4 to 6 Servings

Ⓥ *This is a Vegetarian Recipe* Ⓥ

Ingredients:

- ¼ cup extra-virgin olive oil
- ⅓ cup roasted, unsalted pepitas
- ½ cup pomegranate seeds
- ¾ cup fresh parsley leaves
- 1 small shallot, minced
- 1 teaspoon za'atar

- 2 tablespoons honey
- 2 tablespoons lemon juice
- 3 pounds butternut squash, peeled, seeded, and cut into ½-inch pieces (8 cups)
- Salt and pepper

Directions:

1. Place oven rack to lowest position and pre-heat your oven to 450 degrees. Toss squash with 1 tablespoon oil and sprinkle with salt and pepper. Arrange squash in one layer in rimmed baking sheet and roast until thoroughly browned and tender, 30 to 35 minutes, stirring halfway through roasting. Sprinkle squash with za'atar and allow to cool for about fifteen minutes.
2. Beat shallot, lemon juice, honey, and ¼ teaspoon salt together in a big container. Whisking continuously, slowly drizzle in remaining 3 tablespoons oil. Put in squash, parsley, and pepitas and gently toss to coat. Arrange salad on serving platter and drizzle with pomegranate seeds. Serve.

Tomato Mix Salad

Yield: 6 Servings

⚡ This recipe can be made quickly ⚡

Ⓥ *This is a Vegetarian Recipe* Ⓥ

Ingredients:

- ¼ cup plain Greek yogurt
- 1 garlic clove, minced
- 1 scallion, sliced thin
- 1 tablespoon extra-virgin olive oil
- 1 tablespoon lemon juice
- 1 tablespoon minced fresh oregano
- 1 teaspoon ground cumin

- 2½ pounds ripe tomatoes, cored and cut into ½-inch-thick wedges
- 3 ounces feta cheese, crumbled (¾ cup)
- Salt and pepper

Directions:

1. Toss tomatoes with ½ teaspoon salt and allow to drain using a colander set over bowl for fifteen to twenty minutes.
2. Microwave oil, garlic, and cumin in a container until aromatic, approximately half a minute; allow to cool slightly. Move 1 tablespoon tomato liquid to big container; discard remaining liquid. Beat in yogurt, lemon juice, scallion, oregano, and oil mixture until combined. Put in tomatoes and feta and gently toss to coat. Sprinkle with salt and pepper to taste. Serve.

Tomato-Burrata Mix Salad

Yield: 4 to 6 Servings

Ⓥ *This is a Vegetarian Recipe* Ⓥ

Ingredients:

- ½ cup chopped fresh basil
- 1 garlic clove, minced
- 1 shallot, halved and sliced thin
- 1½ pounds ripe tomatoes, cored and cut into 1-inch pieces
- 1½ tablespoons white balsamic vinegar
- 3 ounces rustic Italian bread, cut into 1-inch pieces (1 cup)
- 6 tablespoons extra-virgin olive oil
- 8 ounces burrata cheese, room temperature
- 8 ounces ripe cherry tomatoes, halved
- Salt and pepper

Directions:

1. Toss tomatoes with ¼ teaspoon salt and allow to drain using a colander for 30 minutes.
2. Pulse bread using a food processor into large crumbs measuring between ⅛ and ¼ inch, approximately ten pulses. Mix crumbs, 2 tablespoons oil, pinch salt, and pinch pepper in 12-inch non-stick skillet. Cook on moderate heat, stirring frequently, until crumbs are crisp and golden, about 10 minutes. Clear center of skillet, put in garlic, and cook, mashing it into skillet, until aromatic, approximately half a minute. Stir garlic into crumbs. Move to plate and allow to cool slightly.
3. Beat shallot, vinegar, and ¼ teaspoon salt together in a big container. Whisking continuously, slowly drizzle in remaining ¼ cup oil. Put in tomatoes and basil and gently toss to combine. Sprinkle with salt and pepper to taste and arrange on serving platter. Cut buratta into 1-inch pieces, collecting creamy liquid. Sprinkle burrata over tomatoes and drizzle with creamy liquid. Sprinkle with bread crumbs and serve instantly.

Tomato-Tuna Mix Salad

Yield: 6 Servings

⚞ This recipe can be made quickly ⚟

Ingredients:

- ¼ cup capers, rinsed and minced
- ¼ cup extra-virgin olive oil
- ¼ cup finely chopped red onion
- ⅓ cup pitted kalamata olives, chopped coarse
- 1 (5-ounce) can solid white tuna in water, drained and flaked
- 1 tablespoon lemon juice
- 2 tablespoons chopped fresh parsley
- 2½ pounds ripe tomatoes, cored and cut into ½-inch-thick wedges
- Salt and pepper

Directions:

1. Toss tomatoes with ½ teaspoon salt and allow to drain using a colander set over bowl for fifteen to twenty minutes.
2. Move 1 tablespoon tomato liquid to big container; discard remaining liquid. Beat in oil, olives, capers, onion, parsley, and lemon juice until combined. Put in tomatoes and tuna and gently toss to coat. Sprinkle with salt and pepper to taste. Serve.

Yogurt-Mint Cucumber Salad

Yield: 4 Servings

Ⓥ This is a Vegetarian Recipe Ⓥ

Ingredients:

- ¼ cup minced fresh mint
- ½ teaspoon ground cumin
- 1 cup plain low-fat yogurt
- 1 garlic clove, minced
- 1 small red onion, sliced thin
- 2 tablespoons extra-virgin olive oil
- 3 cucumbers, peeled, halved along the length, seeded, and sliced ¼ inch thick
- Salt and pepper

Directions:

1. Toss cucumbers and onion with 1 tablespoon salt using a colander set over big container. Weight cucumber-onion mixture with 1 gallon-size zipper-lock bag filled with water; drain for 1 to three hours. Wash and pat dry.
2. Beat yogurt, mint, oil, garlic, and cumin together in a big container. Put in cucumber-onion mixture and toss to coat. Sprinkle with salt and pepper to taste. Serve at room temperature or chilled within one hour.

Zucchini Parmesan Salad

Yield: 6 to 8 Servings

⚡ This recipe can be made quickly ⚡

Ⓥ This is a Vegetarian Recipe Ⓥ

Ingredients:

- ¼ cup lemon juice (2 lemons)
- ½ cup extra-virgin olive oil
- 1½ pounds small zucchini, trimmed and sliced along the length into ribbons
- 2 tablespoons minced fresh mint
- 6 ounces Parmesan cheese, shaved
- Salt and pepper

Directions:

1. Gently toss zucchini with salt and pepper to taste, then arrange beautifully on serving platter.
2. Sprinkle with oil and lemon juice, then drizzle with Parmesan and mint. Serve instantly.

Bonus: Rice and Grain Recipes

Grains are a staple in the Mediterranean diet.

Aromatic Baked Brown Rice

Yield: 4 to 6 Servings

V This is a Vegetarian Recipe V

Ingredients:

- ½ cup minced fresh parsley
- ¾ cup jarred roasted red peppers, rinsed, patted dry, and chopped
- 1 cup chicken or vegetable broth
- 1½ cups long-grain brown rice, rinsed
- 2 onions, chopped fine
- 2¼ cups water
- 4 teaspoons extra-virgin olive oil
- Grated Parmesan cheese
- Lemon wedges
- Salt and pepper

Directions:

1. Place the oven rack in the centre of the oven and pre-heat your oven to 375 degrees. Heat oil in a Dutch oven on moderate heat until it starts to shimmer. Put in onions and 1 teaspoon salt and cook, stirring intermittently, till they become tender and well browned, 12 to 14 minutes.
2. Mix in water and broth and bring to boil. Mix in rice, cover, and move pot to oven. Bake until rice becomes soft and liquid is absorbed, 65 to 70 minutes.
3. Remove pot from oven. Sprinkle red peppers over rice, cover, and allow to sit for about five minutes. Put in parsley to rice and fluff gently with fork to combine. Sprinkle with salt and pepper to taste. Serve with grated Parmesan and lemon wedges.

Aromatic Barley Pilaf

Yield: 4 to 6 Servings

V This is a Vegetarian Recipe V

Ingredients:

- ¼ cup minced fresh parsley
- 1 small onion, chopped fine
- 1½ cups pearl barley, rinsed
- 1½ teaspoons lemon juice
- 1½ teaspoons minced fresh thyme or ½ teaspoon dried
- 2 garlic cloves, minced
- 2 tablespoons minced fresh chives
- 2½ cups water
- 3 tablespoons extra-virgin olive oil
- Salt and pepper

Directions:

1. Heat oil in a big saucepan on moderate heat until it starts to shimmer. Put in onion and ½ teaspoon salt and cook till they become tender, approximately five minutes. Mix in barley, garlic, and thyme and cook, stirring often, until barley is lightly toasted and aromatic, approximately three minutes.
2. Mix in water and bring to simmer. Decrease heat to low, cover, and simmer until barley becomes soft and water is absorbed, 20 to 40 minutes.
3. Remove from the heat, lay clean dish towel underneath lid and let pilaf sit for about ten minutes. Put in parsley, chives, and lemon juice to pilaf and fluff gently with fork to combine. Sprinkle with salt and pepper to taste. Serve.

Basmati Rice Pilaf Mix

Yield: 4 to 6 Servings

Ⓥ This is a Vegetarian Recipe Ⓥ

Ingredients:

- ¼ cup currants

- ¼ cup sliced almonds, toasted
- ¼ teaspoon ground cinnamon
- ½ teaspoon ground turmeric
- 1 small onion, chopped fine
- 1 tablespoon extra-virgin olive oil
- 1½ cups basmati rice, rinsed
- 2 garlic cloves, minced
- 2¼ cups water
- Salt and pepper

Directions:

1. Heat oil in a big saucepan on moderate heat until it starts to shimmer. Put in onion and ¼ teaspoon salt and cook till they become tender, approximately five minutes. Put in rice, garlic, turmeric, and cinnamon and cook, stirring often, until grain edges begin to turn translucent, approximately three minutes.
2. Mix in water and bring to simmer. Decrease heat to low, cover, and simmer gently until rice becomes soft and water is absorbed, 16 to 18 minutes.
3. Remove from the heat, drizzle currants over pilaf. Cover, laying clean dish towel underneath lid, and let pilaf sit for about ten minutes. Put in almonds to pilaf and fluff gently with fork to combine. Sprinkle with salt and pepper to taste. Serve.

Brown Rice Salad with Asparagus, Goat Cheese, and Lemon

Yield: 4 to 6 Servings

Ⓥ This is a Vegetarian Recipe Ⓥ

Ingredients:

- ¼ cup minced fresh parsley
- ¼ cup slivered almonds, toasted

- 1 pound asparagus, trimmed and cut into 1-inch lengths
- 1 shallot, minced
- 1 teaspoon grated lemon zest plus 3 tablespoons juice
- 1½ cups long-grain brown rice
- 2 ounces goat cheese, crumbled (½ cup)
- 3½ tablespoons extra-virgin olive oil
- Salt and pepper

Directions:

1. Bring 4 quarts water to boil in a Dutch oven. Put in rice and 1½ teaspoons salt and cook, stirring intermittently, until rice is tender, about half an hour. Drain rice, spread onto rimmed baking sheet, and drizzle with 1 tablespoon lemon juice. Allow it to cool completely, about fifteen minutes.
2. Heat 1 tablespoon oil in 12-inch frying pan on high heat until just smoking. Put in asparagus, ¼ teaspoon salt, and ¼ teaspoon pepper and cook, stirring intermittently, until asparagus is browned and crisp-tender, about 4 minutes; move to plate and allow to cool slightly.
3. Beat remaining 2½ tablespoons oil, lemon zest and remaining 2 tablespoons juice, shallot, ½ teaspoon salt, and ½ teaspoon pepper together in a big container. Put in rice, asparagus, 2 tablespoons goat cheese, 3 tablespoons almonds, and 3 tablespoons parsley. Gently toss to combine and allow to sit for about ten minutes. Sprinkle with salt and pepper to taste. Move to serving platter and drizzle with remaining 2 tablespoons goat cheese, remaining 1 tablespoon almonds, and remaining 1 tablespoon parsley. Serve.

Carrot-Almond-Bulgur Salad

Yield: 4 to 6 Servings

Ⓥ This is a Vegetarian Recipe Ⓥ

Ingredients:

- ⅛ teaspoon cayenne pepper
- ⅓ cup chopped fresh cilantro
- ⅓ cup chopped fresh mint
- ⅓ cup extra-virgin olive oil
- ½ cup sliced almonds, toasted
- ½ teaspoon ground cumin
- 1 cup water
- 1½ cups medium-grind bulgur, rinsed
- 3 scallions, sliced thin
- 4 carrots, peeled and shredded
- 6 tablespoons lemon juice (2 lemons)
- Salt and pepper

Directions:

1. Mix bulgur, water, ¼ cup lemon juice, and ¼ teaspoon salt in a container. Cover and allow to sit at room temperature until grains are softened and liquid is fully absorbed, about 1½ hours.
2. Beat remaining 2 tablespoons lemon juice, oil, cumin, cayenne, and ½ teaspoon salt together in a big container. Put in bulgur, carrots, scallions, almonds, mint, and cilantro and gently toss to combine. Sprinkle with salt and pepper to taste. Serve.

Chickpea-Spinach-Bulgur

Yield: 4 to 6 Servings

Ⓥ *This is a Vegetarian Recipe* Ⓥ

Ingredients:

- ¾ cup chicken or vegetable broth
- ¾ cup water
- 1 (15-ounce) can chickpeas, rinsed
- 1 cup medium-grind bulgur, rinsed
- 1 onion, chopped fine
- 1 tablespoon lemon juice

- 2 tablespoons za'atar
- 3 garlic cloves, minced
- 3 ounces (3 cups) baby spinach, chopped
- 3 tablespoons extra-virgin olive oil
- Salt and pepper

Directions:

1. Heat 2 tablespoons oil in a big saucepan on moderate heat until it starts to shimmer. Put in onion and ½ teaspoon salt and cook till they become tender, approximately five minutes. Mix in garlic and 1 tablespoon za'atar and cook until aromatic, approximately half a minute.
2. Mix in bulgur, chickpeas, broth, and water and bring to simmer. Decrease heat to low, cover, and simmer gently until bulgur is tender, 16 to 18 minutes.
3. Remove from the heat, lay clean dish towel underneath lid and let bulgur sit for about ten minutes. Put in spinach, lemon juice, remaining 1 tablespoon za'atar, and residual 1 tablespoon oil and fluff gently with fork to combine. Sprinkle with salt and pepper to taste. Serve.

Classic Baked Brown Rice

Yield: 4 Servings

Ⓥ This is a Vegetarian Recipe Ⓥ

Ingredients:

- 1½ cups long-grain brown rice, rinsed
- 2 teaspoons extra-virgin olive oil
- 2⅓ cups boiling water
- Salt and pepper

Directions:

1. Place the oven rack in the centre of the oven and pre-heat your oven to 375 degrees. Mix boiling water, rice, oil, and ½ teaspoon salt in 8-inch square baking dish.
2. Cover dish tightly using double layer of aluminium foil. Bake until rice becomes soft and water is absorbed, about 1 hour. Remove dish from oven, uncover, and gently fluff rice with fork, scraping up any rice that has stuck to bottom. Cover dish with clean dish towel and let rice sit for about five minutes. Uncover and let rice sit for about five minutes longer.
3. Sprinkle with salt and pepper to taste. Serve.

Classic Italian Seafood Risotto

Yield: 4 to 6 Servings

Ingredients:

- ⅛ teaspoon saffron threads, crumbled
- 1 (14.5-ounce) can diced tomatoes, drained
- 1 cup dry white wine
- 1 onion, chopped fine
- 1 tablespoon lemon juice
- 1 teaspoon minced fresh thyme or ¼ teaspoon dried
- 12 ounces large shrimp (26 to 30 per pound), peeled and deveined, shells reserved
- 12 ounces small bay scallops
- 2 bay leaves
- 2 cups Arborio rice
- 2 cups chicken broth
- 2 tablespoons minced fresh parsley
- 2½ cups water
- 4 (8-ounce) bottles clam juice
- 5 garlic cloves, minced
- 5 tablespoons extra-virgin olive oil
- Salt and pepper

Directions:

1. Bring shrimp shells, broth, water, clam juice, tomatoes, and bay leaves to boil in a big saucepan on moderate to high heat. Decrease the heat to a simmer and cook for 20 minutes. Strain mixture through fine-mesh strainer into big container, pressing on solids to extract as much liquid as possible; discard solids. Return broth to now-empty saucepan, cover, and keep warm on low heat.
2. Heat 2 tablespoons oil in a Dutch oven on moderate heat until it starts to shimmer. Put in onion and cook till they become tender, approximately five minutes. Put in rice, garlic, thyme, and saffron and cook, stirring often, until grain edges begin to turn translucent, approximately three minutes.
3. Put in wine and cook, stirring often, until fully absorbed, approximately three minutes. Mix in 3½ cups warm broth, bring to simmer, and cook, stirring intermittently, until almost fully absorbed, about fifteen minutes.
4. Carry on cooking rice, stirring often and adding warm broth, 1 cup at a time, every few minutes as liquid is absorbed, until rice is creamy and cooked through but still somewhat firm in center, about fifteen minutes.
5. Mix in shrimp and scallops and cook, stirring often, until opaque throughout, approximately three minutes. Remove pot from heat, cover, and allow to sit for about five minutes. Adjust consistency with remaining warm broth as required (you may have broth left over). Mix in remaining 3 tablespoons oil, parsley, and lemon juice and sprinkle with salt and pepper to taste. Serve.

Classic Stovetop White Rice

Yield: 4 to 6 Servings

⚡ *This recipe can be made quickly* ⚡

Ⓥ *This is a Vegetarian Recipe* Ⓥ

Ingredients:

- 1 tablespoon extra-virgin olive oil
- 2 cups long-grain white rice, rinsed
- 3 cups water
- Basmati, jasmine, or Texmati rice can be substituted for the long-grain rice.
- Salt and pepper

Directions:

1. Heat oil in a big saucepan on moderate heat until it starts to shimmer. Put in rice and cook, stirring frequently, until grain edges begin to turn translucent, approximately two minutes.
2. Put in water and 1 teaspoon salt and bring to simmer. Cover, decrease the heat to low, and simmer gently until rice becomes soft and water is absorbed, approximately twenty minutes. Remove from the heat, lay clean dish towel underneath lid and let rice sit for about ten minutes. Gently fluff rice with fork. Sprinkle with salt and pepper to taste. Serve.

Classic Tabbouleh

Yield: 4 to 6 Servings

Ⓥ This is a Vegetarian Recipe Ⓥ

Ingredients:

- ⅛ teaspoon cayenne pepper
- ¼ cup lemon juice (2 lemons)
- ½ cup medium-grind bulgur, rinsed
- ½ cup minced fresh mint
- 1½ cups minced fresh parsley
- 2 scallions, sliced thin
- 3 tomatoes, cored and cut into ½-inch pieces
- 6 tablespoons extra-virgin olive oil

- Salt and pepper

Directions:

1. Toss tomatoes with ¼ teaspoon salt using a fine-mesh strainer set over bowl and let drain, tossing occasionally, for 30 minutes; reserve 2 tablespoons drained tomato juice. Toss bulgur with 2 tablespoons lemon juice and reserved tomato juice in a container and allow to sit until grains start to become tender, 30 to 40 minutes.
2. Beat remaining 2 tablespoons lemon juice, oil, cayenne, and ¼ teaspoon salt together in a big container. Put in tomatoes, bulgur, parsley, mint, and scallions and toss gently to combine. Cover and allow to sit at room temperature until flavors have blended and bulgur is tender, about 1 hour. Before serving, toss salad to recombine and sprinkle with salt and pepper to taste.

Farro Cucumber-Mint Salad

Yield: 4 to 6 Servings

Ⓥ *This is a Vegetarian Recipe* Ⓥ

Ingredients:

- 1 cup baby arugula
- 1 English cucumber, halved along the length, seeded, and cut into ¼-inch pieces
- 1½ cups whole farro
- 2 tablespoons lemon juice
- 2 tablespoons minced shallot
- 2 tablespoons plain Greek yogurt
- 3 tablespoons chopped fresh mint
- 3 tablespoons extra-virgin olive oil
- 6 ounces cherry tomatoes, halved
- Salt and pepper

Directions:

1. Bring 4 quarts water to boil in a Dutch oven. Put in farro and 1 tablespoon salt, return to boil, and cook until grains are soft with slight chew, 15 to 30 minutes. Drain farro, spread in rimmed baking sheet, and allow to cool completely, about fifteen minutes.
2. Beat oil, lemon juice, shallot, yogurt, ¼ teaspoon salt, and ¼ teaspoon pepper together in a big container. Put in farro, cucumber, tomatoes, arugula, and mint and toss gently to combine. Sprinkle with salt and pepper to taste. Serve.

Farro Salad Mix

Yield: 4 to 6 Servings

Ⓥ *This is a Vegetarian Recipe* Ⓥ

Ingredients:

- 1 teaspoon Dijon mustard
- 1½ cups whole farro
- 2 ounces feta cheese, crumbled (½ cup)
- 2 tablespoons lemon juice
- 2 tablespoons minced shallot
- 3 tablespoons chopped fresh dill
- 3 tablespoons extra-virgin olive oil
- 6 ounces asparagus, trimmed and cut into 1-inch lengths
- 6 ounces cherry tomatoes, halved
- 6 ounces sugar snap peas, strings removed, cut into 1-inch lengths
- Salt and pepper

Directions:

1. Bring 4 quarts water to boil in a Dutch oven. Put in asparagus, snap peas, and 1 tablespoon salt and cook until crisp-tender,

approximately three minutes. Use a slotted spoon to move vegetables to large plate and allow to cool completely, about fifteen minutes.

2. Put in farro to water, return to boil, and cook until grains are soft with slight chew, 15 to 30 minutes. Drain farro, spread in rimmed baking sheet, and allow to cool completely, about fifteen minutes.

3. Beat oil, lemon juice, shallot, mustard, ¼ teaspoon salt, and ¼ teaspoon pepper together in a big container. Put in vegetables, farro, tomatoes, dill, and ¼ cup feta and toss gently to combine. Sprinkle with salt and pepper to taste. Move to serving platter and drizzle with remaining ¼ cup feta. Serve.

Farrotto Mix

Yield: 6 Servings

Ingredients:

- ½ onion, chopped fine
- 1 cup frozen peas, thawed
- 1 garlic clove, minced
- 1 tablespoon minced fresh chives
- 1 teaspoon grated lemon zest plus 1 teaspoon juice
- 1½ cups whole farro
- 1½ ounces Parmesan cheese, grated (¾ cup)
- 2 tablespoons extra-virgin olive oil
- 2 teaspoons minced fresh tarragon
- 3 cups chicken broth
- 3 cups water
- 4 ounces asparagus, trimmed and cut on bias into 1-inch lengths
- 4 ounces pancetta, cut into ¼-inch pieces
- Salt and pepper

Directions:

1. Pulse farro using a blender until about half of grains are broken into smaller pieces, about 6 pulses.
2. Bring broth and water to boil in moderate-sized saucepan on high heat. Put in asparagus and cook until crisp-tender, 2 to 3 minutes. Use a slotted spoon to move asparagus to a container and set aside. Decrease heat to low, cover broth mixture, and keep warm.
3. Cook pancetta in a Dutch oven on moderate heat until lightly browned and fat has rendered, approximately five minutes. Put in 1 tablespoon oil and onion and cook till they become tender, approximately five minutes. Mix in garlic and cook until aromatic, approximately half a minute. Put in farro and cook, stirring often, until grains are lightly toasted, approximately three minutes.
4. Stir 5 cups warm broth mixture into farro mixture, decrease the heat to low, cover, and cook until almost all liquid has been absorbed and farro is just al dente, about 25 minutes, stirring twice during cooking.
5. Put in peas, tarragon, ¾ teaspoon salt, and ½ teaspoon pepper and cook, stirring continuously, until farro becomes creamy, approximately five minutes. Remove from the heat, mix in Parmesan, chives, lemon zest and juice, remaining 1 tablespoon oil, and reserved asparagus. Adjust consistency with remaining warm broth mixture as required (you may have broth left over). Sprinkle with salt and pepper to taste. Serve.

Fennel-Parmesan Farro

Yield: 4 to 6 Servings

Ⓥ *This is a Vegetarian Recipe* Ⓥ

Ingredients:

- ¼ cup minced fresh parsley
- 1 onion, chopped fine
- 1 ounce Parmesan cheese, grated (½ cup)

- 1 small fennel bulb, stalks discarded, bulb halved, cored, and chopped fine
- 1 teaspoon minced fresh thyme or ¼ teaspoon dried
- 1½ cups whole farro
- 2 teaspoons sherry vinegar
- 3 garlic cloves, minced
- 3 tablespoons extra-virgin olive oil
- Salt and pepper

Directions:

1. Bring 4 quarts water to boil in a Dutch oven. Put in farro and 1 tablespoon salt, return to boil, and cook until grains are soft with slight chew, 15 to 30 minutes. Drain farro, return to now-empty pot, and cover to keep warm.
2. Heat 2 tablespoons oil in 12-inch frying pan on moderate heat until it starts to shimmer. Put in onion, fennel, and ¼ teaspoon salt and cook, stirring intermittently, till they become tender, eight to ten minutes. Put in garlic and thyme and cook until aromatic, approximately half a minute.
3. Put in residual 1 tablespoon oil and farro and cook, stirring often, until heated through, approximately two minutes. Remove from the heat, mix in Parmesan, parsley, and vinegar. Sprinkle with salt and pepper to taste. Serve.

Feta-Grape-Bulgur Salad with Grapes and Feta

Yield: 4 to 6 Servings

Ⓥ This is a Vegetarian Recipe Ⓥ

Ingredients:

- ¼ cup chopped fresh mint
- ¼ cup extra-virgin olive oil

- ¼ teaspoon ground cumin
- ½ cup slivered almonds, toasted
- 1 cup water
- 1½ cups medium-grind bulgur, rinsed
- 2 ounces feta cheese, crumbled (½ cup)
- 2 scallions, sliced thin
- 5 tablespoons lemon juice (2 lemons)
- 6 ounces seedless red grapes, quartered (1 cup)
- Pinch cayenne pepper
- Salt and pepper

Directions:

1. Mix bulgur, water, ¼ cup lemon juice, and ¼ teaspoon salt in a container. Cover and allow to sit at room temperature until grains are softened and liquid is fully absorbed, about 1½ hours.
2. Beat remaining 1 tablespoon lemon juice, oil, cumin, cayenne, and ¼ teaspoon salt together in a big container. Put in bulgur, grapes, ⅓ cup almonds, ⅓ cup feta, scallions, and mint and gently toss to combine. Sprinkle with salt and pepper to taste. Sprinkle with remaining almonds and remaining feta before you serve.

Greek Style Meaty Bulgur

Yield: 4 to 6 Servings

Ingredients:

- ½ cup jarred roasted red peppers, rinsed, patted dry, and chopped
- 1 bay leaf
- 1 cup medium-grind bulgur, rinsed
- 1 onion, chopped fine
- 1 tablespoon chopped fresh dill
- 1 teaspoon extra-virgin olive oil
- 1⅓ cups vegetable broth

- 2 teaspoons minced fresh marjoram or ½ teaspoon dried
- 3 garlic cloves, minced
- 8 ounces ground lamb
- Lemon wedges
- Salt and pepper

Directions:

1. Heat oil in a big saucepan on moderate to high heat until just smoking. Put in lamb, ½ teaspoon salt, and ¼ teaspoon pepper and cook, breaking up meat with wooden spoon, until browned, 3 to 5 minutes. Mix in onion and red peppers and cook until onion is softened, 5 to 7 minutes. Mix in garlic and marjoram and cook until aromatic, approximately half a minute.
2. Mix in bulgur, broth, and bay leaf and bring to simmer. Decrease heat to low, cover, and simmer gently until bulgur is tender, 16 to 18 minutes.
3. Remove from the heat, lay clean dish towel underneath lid and let bulgur sit for about ten minutes. Put in dill and fluff gently with fork to combine. Sprinkle with salt and pepper to taste. Serve with lemon wedges.

Hearty Barley Mix

Yield: 4 Servings

Ⓥ *This is a Vegetarian Recipe* Ⓥ

Ingredients:

- ⅛ teaspoon ground cardamom
- ½ cup plain yogurt
- ½ teaspoon ground cumin
- ⅔ cup raw sunflower seeds
- ¾ teaspoon ground coriander
- 1 cup pearl barley
- 1½ tablespoons minced fresh mint

- 1½ teaspoons grated lemon zest plus 1½ tablespoons juice
- 3 tablespoons extra-virgin olive oil
- 5 carrots, peeled
- 8 ounces snow peas, strings removed, halved along the length
- Salt and pepper

Directions:

1. Beat yogurt, ½ teaspoon lemon zest and 1½ teaspoons juice, 1½ teaspoons mint, ¼ teaspoon salt, and ⅛ teaspoon pepper together in a small-sized container; cover put inside your fridge until ready to serve.
2. Bring 4 quarts water to boil in a Dutch oven. Put in barley and 1 tablespoon salt, return to boil, and cook until tender, 20 to 40 minutes. Drain barley, return to now-empty pot, and cover to keep warm.
3. In the meantime, halve carrots crosswise, then halve or quarter along the length to create uniformly sized pieces. Heat 1 tablespoon oil in 12-inch frying pan on moderate to high heat until just smoking. Put in carrots and ½ teaspoon coriander and cook, stirring intermittently, until mildly charred and just tender, 5 to 7 minutes. Put in snow peas and cook, stirring intermittently, until spotty brown, 3 to 5 minutes; move to plate.
4. Heat 1½ teaspoons oil in now-empty frying pan on moderate heat until it starts to shimmer. Put in sunflower seeds, cumin, cardamom, remaining ¼ teaspoon coriander, and ¼ teaspoon salt. Cook, stirring continuously, until seeds are toasted, approximately two minutes; move to small-sized container.
5. Beat remaining 1 teaspoon lemon zest and 1 tablespoon juice, remaining 1 tablespoon mint, and remaining 1½ tablespoons oil together in a big container. Put in barley and carrot–snow pea mixture and gently toss to combine. Sprinkle with salt and pepper to taste. Serve, topping individual portions with spiced sunflower seeds and drizzling with yogurt sauce.

Hearty Barley Risotto

Yield: 4 to 6 Servings

Ⓥ *This is a Vegetarian Recipe* Ⓥ

Ingredients:

- 1 carrot, peeled and chopped fine
- 1 cup dry white wine
- 1 onion, chopped fine
- 1 teaspoon minced fresh thyme or ¼ teaspoon dried
- 1½ cups pearl barley
- 2 ounces Parmesan cheese, grated (1 cup)
- 2 tablespoons extra-virgin olive oil
- 4 cups chicken or vegetable broth
- 4 cups water
- Salt and pepper

Directions:

1. Bring broth and water to simmer in moderate-sized saucepan. Decrease heat to low and cover to keep warm.
2. Heat 1 tablespoon oil in a Dutch oven on moderate heat until it starts to shimmer. Put in onion and carrot and cook till they become tender, 5 to 7 minutes. Put in barley and cook, stirring frequently, until lightly toasted and aromatic, about 4 minutes.
3. Put in wine and cook, stirring often, until fully absorbed, approximately two minutes. Mix in 3 cups warm broth and thyme, bring to simmer, and cook, stirring intermittently, until liquid is absorbed and bottom of pot is dry, 22 to 25 minutes. Mix in 2 cups warm broth, bring to simmer, and cook, stirring intermittently, until liquid is absorbed and bottom of pot is dry, fifteen to twenty minutes.
4. Carry on cooking risotto, stirring frequently and adding warm broth as required to stop pot bottom from becoming dry, until barley is cooked through but still somewhat firm in center, fifteen to twenty minutes. Remove from the heat, adjust

consistency with remaining warm broth as required (you may have broth left over). Mix in Parmesan and residual 1 tablespoon oil and sprinkle with salt and pepper to taste. Serve.

Hearty Freekeh Pilaf

Yield: 4 to 6 Servings

Ⓥ *This is a Vegetarian Recipe* Ⓥ

Ingredients:

- ¼ cup chopped fresh mint
- ¼ cup extra-virgin olive oil, plus extra for serving
- ¼ cup shelled pistachios, toasted and coarsely chopped
- ¼ teaspoon ground coriander
- ¼ teaspoon ground cumin
- 1 head cauliflower (2 pounds), cored and cut into ½-inch florets
- 1 shallot, minced
- 1½ cups whole freekeh
- 1½ tablespoons lemon juice
- 1½ teaspoons grated fresh ginger
- 3 ounces pitted dates, chopped (½ cup)
- Salt and pepper

Directions:

1. Bring 4 quarts water to boil in a Dutch oven. Put in freekeh and 1 tablespoon salt, return to boil, and cook until grains are tender, 30 to 45 minutes. Drain freekeh, return to now-empty pot, and cover to keep warm.
2. Heat 2 tablespoons oil in 12-inch non-stick frying pan on moderate to high heat until it starts to shimmer. Put in cauliflower, ½ teaspoon salt, and ¼ teaspoon pepper, cover, and cook until florets are softened and start to brown, approximately five minutes.

3. Remove lid and continue to cook, stirring intermittently, until florets turn spotty brown, about 10 minutes. Put in remaining 2 tablespoons oil, dates, shallot, ginger, coriander, and cumin and cook, stirring often, until dates and shallot are softened and aromatic, approximately three minutes.

4. Decrease heat to low, put in freekeh, and cook, stirring often, until heated through, about 1 minute. Remove from the heat, mix in pistachios, mint, and lemon juice. Sprinkle with salt and pepper to taste and drizzle with extra oil. Serve.

Herby-Lemony Farro

Yield: 4 to 6 Servings

Ⓥ *This is a Vegetarian Recipe* Ⓥ

Ingredients:

- ¼ cup chopped fresh mint
- ¼ cup chopped fresh parsley
- 1 garlic clove, minced
- 1 onion, chopped fine
- 1 tablespoon lemon juice
- 1½ cups whole farro
- 3 tablespoons extra-virgin olive oil
- Salt and pepper

Directions:

1. Bring 4 quarts water to boil in a Dutch oven. Put in farro and 1 tablespoon salt, return to boil, and cook until grains are soft with slight chew, 15 to 30 minutes. Drain farro, return to now-empty pot, and cover to keep warm.

2. Heat 2 tablespoons oil in 12-inch frying pan on moderate heat until it starts to shimmer. Put in onion and ¼ teaspoon salt and cook till they become tender, approximately five minutes. Mix in garlic and cook until aromatic, approximately half a minute.

3. Put in residual 1 tablespoon oil and farro and cook, stirring often, until heated through, approximately two minutes. Remove from the heat, mix in parsley, mint, and lemon juice. Sprinkle with salt and pepper to taste. Serve.

Italian Paniscia

Yield: 8 Servings

Ingredients:

BEANS AND BROTH

- 1 carrot, peeled and chopped fine
- 1 celery rib, chopped fine
- 1 cup shredded red cabbage
- 1 leek, white and light green parts only, halved along the length, chopped fine, and washed thoroughly
- 1 small sprig fresh rosemary
- 1 tablespoon extra-virgin olive oil
- 1 zucchini, cut into ½-inch pieces
- 2 ounces pancetta, chopped fine
- 8 ounces (1¼ cups) dried cranberry beans, picked over and rinsed
- Salt and pepper

RISOTTO

- 1 cup dry red wine
- 1 small onion, chopped fine
- 1 tablespoon tomato paste
- 1½ cups carnaroli rice
- 2 (½-inch-thick) slices salami (6 ounces), cut into ½-inch pieces
- 2 tablespoons extra-virgin olive oil
- 2 teaspoons red wine vinegar
- Salt and pepper

Directions:

1. **FOR THE BEANS AND BROTH:** Dissolve 1½ tablespoons salt in 2 quarts cold water in large container. Put in beans and soak at room temperature for minimum 8 hours or for maximum 24 hours. Drain and wash thoroughly.

2. Heat oil in a big saucepan on moderate to high heat until it starts to shimmer. Put in pancetta and cook, stirring intermittently, until starting to brown, 3 to 5 minutes. Mix in leek, carrot, celery, zucchini, and cabbage and cook till they become tender and lightly browned, 5 to 7 minutes. Mix in drained beans, rosemary, and 8 cups water and bring to boil. Decrease heat to moderate to low, cover, and simmer, stirring intermittently, until beans are soft and liquid begins to thicken, forty to sixty minutes. Strain bean-vegetable mixture through fine-mesh strainer into big container. Discard rosemary and move bean-vegetable mixture to different container; set aside. Return broth to now-empty saucepan, cover, and keep warm on low heat.

3. **FOR THE RISOTTO**: Heat 1 tablespoon oil in a Dutch oven on moderate heat until it starts to shimmer. Put in onion, salami, and ½ teaspoon salt and cook until onion is softened, approximately five minutes. Put in rice and cook, stirring often, until grain edges begin to turn translucent, approximately three minutes.

4. Mix in tomato paste and cook until aromatic, about 1 minute. Put in wine and cook, stirring often, until fully absorbed, approximately two minutes. Mix in 2 cups warm broth, bring to simmer, and cook, stirring intermittently, until almost fully absorbed, approximately five minutes.

5. Carry on cooking rice, stirring often and adding warm broth, 1 cup at a time, every few minutes as liquid is absorbed, until rice is creamy and cooked through but still somewhat firm in center, 14 to 16 minutes.

6. Remove from the heat, mix in bean-vegetable mixture, cover, and allow to sit for about five minutes. Adjust consistency with remaining warm broth as required (you may have broth left over). Mix in residual 1 tablespoon oil and vinegar and sprinkle with salt and pepper to taste. Serve.

Italian Parmesan Farrotto

Yield: 6 Servings

Ⓥ This is a Vegetarian Recipe Ⓥ

Ingredients:

- ½ onion, chopped fine
- 1 garlic clove, minced
- 1½ cups whole farro
- 2 ounces Parmesan cheese, grated (1 cup)
- 2 tablespoons minced fresh parsley
- 2 teaspoons lemon juice
- 2 teaspoons minced fresh thyme
- 3 cups chicken or vegetable broth
- 3 cups water
- 3 tablespoons extra-virgin olive oil
- Salt and pepper

Directions:

1. Pulse farro using a blender until about half of grains are broken into smaller pieces, about 6 pulses.
2. Bring broth and water to boil in moderate-sized saucepan on high heat. Decrease heat to low, cover, and keep warm.
3. Heat 2 tablespoons oil in a Dutch oven over moderate to low heat. Put in onion and cook till they become tender, approximately five minutes. Mix in garlic and cook until aromatic, approximately half a minute. Put in farro and cook, stirring often, until grains are lightly toasted, approximately three minutes.
4. Stir 5 cups warm broth mixture into farro mixture, decrease the heat to low, cover, and cook until almost all liquid has been absorbed and farro is just al dente, about 25 minutes, stirring twice during cooking.
5. Put in thyme, 1 teaspoon salt, and ¾ teaspoon pepper and cook, stirring continuously, until farro becomes creamy, approximately

five minutes. Remove from the heat, mix in Parmesan, parsley, lemon juice, and remaining 1 tablespoon oil. Adjust consistency with remaining warm broth mixture as required (you may have broth left over). Sprinkle with salt and pepper to taste. Serve.

Lebanese Herbed Basmati Rice

Yield: 4 to 6 Servings

Ⓥ *This is a Vegetarian Recipe* Ⓥ

Ingredients:

- 1 garlic clove, minced
- 1 onion, chopped fine
- 1½ cups basmati rice
- 2 ounces vermicelli pasta, broken into 1-inch lengths
- 2½ cups chicken or vegetable broth
- 3 tablespoons extra-virgin olive oil
- 3 tablespoons minced fresh parsley
- Salt and pepper

Directions:

1. Put rice in a moderate-sized container and cover with hot tap water by 2 inches; allow to stand for about fifteen minutes.
2. Use your hands to lightly rinse the grains to eliminate the surplus stach. Cautiously drain water, leaving rice in a container. Pour cold tap water into the rice and drain water. Repeat the process of pouring in and draining cold water 4 to 5 times, until water runs nearly transparent. Drain rice using a fine-mesh strainer.
3. Heat oil in a big saucepan on moderate heat until it starts to shimmer. Put in pasta and cook, stirring intermittently, until browned, approximately three minutes. Put in onion and garlic and cook, stirring intermittently, until onion becomes tender but not browned, about 4 minutes. Put in rice and cook, stirring intermittently, until edges of rice begin to turn translucent,

approximately three minutes. Put in broth and 1¼ teaspoons salt and bring to boil. Decrease heat to low, cover, and simmer gently until rice and pasta are soft and broth is absorbed, about 10 minutes. Remove from the heat, lay clean dish towel underneath lid and let pilaf sit for about ten minutes. Put in parsley to pilaf and fluff gently with fork to combine. Sprinkle with salt and pepper to taste. Serve.

Mushroom-Bulgur Pilaf

Yield: 4 Servings

Ⓥ *This is a Vegetarian Recipe* Ⓥ

Ingredients:

- ¼ cup minced fresh parsley
- ¼ ounce dried porcini mushrooms, rinsed and minced
- ¾ cup chicken or vegetable broth
- ¾ cup water
- 1 cup medium-grind bulgur, rinsed
- 1 onion, chopped fine
- 2 garlic cloves, minced
- 2 tablespoons extra-virgin olive oil
- 8 ounces cremini mushrooms, trimmed, halved if small or quartered if large
- Salt and pepper

Directions:

1. Heat oil in a big saucepan on moderate heat until it starts to shimmer. Put in onion, porcini mushrooms, and ½ teaspoon salt and cook until onion is softened, approximately five minutes. Mix in cremini mushrooms, increase heat to medium-high, cover, and cook until cremini release their liquid and begin to brown, about 4 minutes. Mix in garlic and cook until aromatic, approximately half a minute.

2. Mix in bulgur, broth, and water and bring to simmer. Decrease heat to low, cover, and simmer gently until bulgur is tender, 16 to 18 minutes.

3. Remove from the heat, lay clean dish towel underneath lid and let pilaf sit for about ten minutes. Put in parsley to pilaf and fluff gently with fork to combine. Sprinkle with salt and pepper to taste. Serve.

Mushroom-Thyme Farro

Yield: 4 to 6 Servings

Ⓥ This is a Vegetarian Recipe Ⓥ

Ingredients:

- 1 shallot, minced
- 1½ cups whole farro
- 1½ teaspoons minced fresh thyme or ½ teaspoon dried
- 1½ teaspoons sherry vinegar, plus extra for serving
- 12 ounces cremini mushrooms, trimmed and chopped coarse
- 3 tablespoons dry sherry
- 3 tablespoons extra-virgin olive oil
- 3 tablespoons minced fresh parsley
- Salt and pepper

Directions:

1. Bring 4 quarts water to boil in a Dutch oven. Put in farro and 1 tablespoon salt, return to boil, and cook until grains are soft with slight chew, 15 to 30 minutes. Drain farro, return to now-empty pot, and cover to keep warm.

2. Heat 2 tablespoons oil in 12-inch frying pan on moderate heat until it starts to shimmer. Put in mushrooms, shallot, thyme, and ¼ teaspoon salt and cook, stirring intermittently, until moisture has evaporated and vegetables start to brown, eight to ten

minutes. Mix in sherry and cook, scraping up any browned bits, until frying pan is almost dry.

3. Put in residual 1 tablespoon oil and farro and cook, stirring often, until heated through, approximately two minutes. Remove from the heat, mix in parsley and vinegar. Sprinkle with salt, pepper, and extra vinegar to taste and serve.

North African Spiced Baked Rice

Yield: 6 to 8 Servings

Ⓥ This is a Vegetarian Recipe Ⓥ

Ingredients:

- ¼ cup extra-virgin olive oil
- ¾ cup large pitted brine-cured green olives, halved
- 1 fennel bulb, stalks discarded, bulb halved, cored, and chopped fine
- 1 small onion, chopped fine
- 1½ cups long-grain white rice, rinsed
- 1½ pounds sweet potatoes, peeled and cut into 1-inch pieces
- 2 tablespoons minced fresh cilantro
- 2 teaspoons ras el hanout
- 2¾ cups chicken or vegetable broth
- 4 garlic cloves, minced
- Lime wedges
- Salt and pepper

Directions:

1. Place the oven rack in the centre of the oven and pre-heat your oven to 400 degrees. Toss potatoes with 2 tablespoons oil and ½ teaspoon salt. Lay out the potatoes in one layer in rimmed baking sheet and roast until soft and browned, about half an hour, stirring potatoes halfway through roasting. Take the

    potatoes out of the oven and decrease oven temperature to 350 degrees.

2. Heat remaining 2 tablespoons oil in a Dutch oven on moderate heat until it starts to shimmer. Put in fennel and onion and cook till they become tender, 5 to 7 minutes. Mix in rice, garlic, and ras el hanout and cook, stirring often, until grain edges begin to turn translucent, approximately three minutes.

3. Mix in broth and olives and bring to boil. Cover, move pot to oven, and bake until rice becomes soft and liquid is absorbed, 12 to fifteen minutes.

4. Remove pot from oven and allow to sit for about ten minutes. Put in potatoes to rice and fluff gently with fork to combine. Sprinkle with salt and pepper to taste. Sprinkle with cilantro and serve with lime wedges.

Nutty Freekeh Salad

Yield: 4 to 6 Servings

Ⓥ This is a Vegetarian Recipe Ⓥ

Ingredients:

- ⅓ cup golden raisins
- ⅓ cup walnuts, toasted and chopped
- ½ cup Tahini-Lemon Dressing
- ½ teaspoon ground fenugreek
- 1 cup coarsely chopped cilantro
- 1 tablespoon extra-virgin olive oil
- 1½ cups whole freekeh
- 1½ pounds butternut squash, peeled, seeded, and cut into ½-inch pieces (4 cups)
- Salt and pepper

Directions:

1. Place oven rack on the lowest position and pre-heat your oven to 450 degrees. Toss squash with oil and fenugreek and sprinkle with salt and pepper. Arrange squash in one layer in rimmed baking sheet and roast until thoroughly browned and tender, 30 to 35 minutes, stirring halfway through roasting; allow to cool to room temperature.

2. In the meantime, bring 4 quarts water to boil in a Dutch oven. Put in freekeh and 1 tablespoon salt, return to boil, and cook until grains are tender, 30 to 45 minutes. Drain freekeh, move to big container, and allow to cool completely, about fifteen minutes.

3. Mix raisins and ¼ cup hot tap water in a small-sized container and allow to sit till they become tender, approximately five minutes; drain raisins. Put in squash, raisins, dressing, cilantro, and walnuts to a container with freekeh and gently toss to combine. Sprinkle with salt and pepper to taste. Serve.

Nutty Wheat Berry Salad

Yield: 4 to 6 Servings

Ⓥ This is a Vegetarian Recipe Ⓥ

Ingredients:

- ¼ cup pine nuts, toasted
- ½ cup fresh parsley leaves
- 1 small shallot, minced
- 1 teaspoon Dijon mustard
- 1 teaspoon honey
- 1½ cups wheat berries
- 2 ounces goat cheese, crumbled (½ cup)
- 2 tablespoons balsamic vinegar
- 3 tablespoons extra-virgin olive oil
- 8 ounces figs, cut into ½-inch pieces
- Salt and pepper

Directions:

1. Bring 4 quarts water to boil in a Dutch oven. Put in wheat berries and 1½ teaspoons salt, return to boil, and cook until soft but still chewy, 60 to 70 minutes. Drain wheat berries, spread onto rimmed baking sheet, and allow to cool completely, about fifteen minutes.
2. Beat vinegar, shallot, mustard, honey, ¼ teaspoon salt, and ¼ teaspoon pepper together in a big container. Whisking continuously, slowly drizzle in oil. Put in wheat berries, figs, parsley, and pine nuts and toss gently to combine. Sprinkle with salt and pepper to taste. Move to serving platter and drizzle with goat cheese. Serve.

Rich Italian Parmesan Polenta

Yield: 4 to 6 Servings

Ⓥ This is a Vegetarian Recipe Ⓥ

Ingredients:

- 1½ cups coarse-ground cornmeal
- 2 ounces Parmesan cheese, grated (1 cup), plus extra for serving
- 2 tablespoons extra-virgin olive oil
- 7½ cups water
- Pinch baking soda
- Salt and pepper

Directions:

1. Bring water to boil in a big saucepan on moderate to high heat. Mix in 1½ teaspoons salt and baking soda. Slowly pour cornmeal

into water gradually while stirring back and forth with wooden spoon or rubber spatula. Bring mixture to boil, stirring continuously, about 1 minute. Decrease heat to lowest setting and cover.

2. After 5 minutes, beat polenta to smooth out any lumps that may have formed, approximately fifteen seconds. (Make sure to scrape down sides and bottom of saucepan.) Cover and continue to cook, without stirring, until polenta grains are soft but slightly al dente, about 25 minutes longer. (Polenta should be loose and barely hold its shape; it will continue to thicken as it cools.)

3. Remove from the heat, mix in Parmesan and oil and season with pepper to taste. Cover and allow to sit for about five minutes. Serve, passing extra Parmesan separately.

Sautéed Cherry Tomato And Fresh Mozzarella Polenta Topping

Yield: enough for 4 to 6 servings

Ⓥ This is a Vegetarian Recipe Ⓥ

Ingredients:

- 1½ pounds cherry tomatoes, halved
- 2 garlic cloves, sliced thin
- 2 tablespoons shredded fresh basil
- 3 ounces fresh mozzarella cheese, shredded (¾ cup)
- 3 tablespoons extra-virgin olive oil
- Pinch red pepper flakes
- Pinch sugar
- Salt and pepper

Directions:

1. Cook oil, garlic, pepper flakes, and sugar in 12-inch non-stick frying pan on moderate to high heat until aromatic and sizzling, about 1 minute. Mix in tomatoes and cook until just starting to soften, about 1 minute.

2. Sprinkle with salt and pepper to taste. Spoon mixture over individual portions of polenta and top with mozzarella and basil. Serve.

BROCCOLI RABE, SUN-DRIED TOMATO, AND PINE NUT TOPPING

Yield: enough for 4 to 6 servings

Ⓥ *This is a Vegetarian Recipe* Ⓥ

Ingredients:

- ¼ cup chicken or vegetable broth
- ¼ cup grated Parmesan cheese
- ½ cup oil-packed sun-dried tomatoes, chopped coarse
- ½ teaspoon red pepper flakes
- 1 pound broccoli rabe, trimmed and cut into 1½-inch pieces
- 2 tablespoons pine nuts, toasted
- 3 tablespoons extra-virgin olive oil
- 6 garlic cloves, minced
- Broccolini can be substituted for the broccoli rabe.
- Salt and pepper

Directions:

1. Cook sun-dried tomatoes, oil, garlic, pepper flakes, and ½ teaspoon salt in 12-inch non-stick frying pan on moderate to high heat, stirring often, until garlic is aromatic and slightly toasted, approximately two minutes. Put in broccoli rabe and broth, cover, and cook until broccoli rabe turns bright green, approximately two minutes. Uncover and cook, stirring often, until most of broth has evaporated and broccoli rabe is just tender, approximately three minutes.
2. Sprinkle with salt and pepper to taste. Spoon mixture over individual portions of polenta and top with pine nuts and Parmesan. Serve.

Rich Spanish Vegetable Paella

Yield: 6 Servings

Ⓥ This is a Vegetarian Recipe Ⓥ

Ingredients:

- ⅓ cup dry white wine
- ½ cup frozen peas, thawed
- ½ cup pitted kalamata olives, chopped
- ½ teaspoon saffron threads, crumbled
- ½ teaspoon smoked paprika
- 1 (14.5-ounce) can diced tomatoes, drained, minced, and drained again
- 1 fennel bulb, stalks discarded, bulb halved, cored, and sliced thin
- 1 onion, chopped fine
- 2 cups Bomba rice
- 2 red bell peppers, stemmed, seeded, and chopped coarse
- 2 tablespoons lemon juice
- 3 cups jarred whole baby artichokes packed in water, quartered, rinsed, and patted dry
- 3 cups vegetable broth
- 3 tablespoons chopped fresh parsley
- 6 tablespoons extra-virgin olive oil
- 9 garlic cloves, peeled (3 whole, 6 minced)
- Salt and pepper

Directions:

1. Place oven rack to lower-middle position, place rimmed baking sheet on rack, and pre-heat your oven to 450 degrees. Toss artichokes and peppers with olives, whole garlic cloves, 2 tablespoons oil, ½ teaspoon salt, and ¼ teaspoon pepper in a container. Lay out vegetables in hot sheet and roast until

artichokes become browned around edges and peppers become browned, 20 minutes to half an hour; allow to cool slightly.

2. Mince roasted garlic. In big container, beat 2 tablespoons oil, 2 tablespoons parsley, lemon juice, and minced roasted garlic together. Put in roasted vegetables and toss to combine. Sprinkle with salt and pepper to taste.

3. Reduce oven temperature to 350 degrees. Heat remaining 2 tablespoons oil in a Dutch oven on moderate heat until it starts to shimmer. Put in onion and fennel and cook till they become tender, eight to ten minutes.

4. Mix in remaining minced garlic and paprika and cook until aromatic, approximately half a minute. Mix in tomatoes and cook until mixture begins to darken and thicken slightly, approximately three minutes. Mix in rice and cook until grains are well coated with tomato mixture, approximately two minutes. Mix in broth, wine, saffron, and 1 teaspoon salt. Increase heat to medium-high and bring to boil, stirring intermittently. Cover, move pot to oven, and bake until liquid is absorbed and rice is tender, 25 to 35 minutes.

5. For optional socarrat, move pot to stovetop and remove lid. Cook on moderate to high heat for approximately five minutes, rotating pot as required, until bottom layer of rice is thoroughly browned and crisp.

6. Sprinkle roasted vegetables and peas over rice, cover, and let paella sit for about five minutes. Sprinkle with remaining 1 tablespoon parsley and serve.

Spanish Broth Rice

Yield: 4 to 6 Servings

Ingredients:

- ¼ cup minced fresh parsley
- 1 (8-ounce) bottle clam juice
- 1 green bell pepper, stemmed, seeded, and chopped fine

- 1 leek, white and light green parts only, halved along the length, chopped fine, and washed thoroughly
- 1 tablespoon white wine vinegar
- 1½ cups Bomba rice
- 2 cups dry white wine
- 2 pounds littleneck clams, scrubbed
- 5 cups water
- 5 tablespoons extra-virgin olive oil
- 6 garlic cloves, minced
- Lemon wedges
- Salt and pepper

Directions:

1. Mix 3 tablespoons oil, parsley, half of garlic, and vinegar in a container; set aside. Bring wine to boil in a big saucepan on high heat. Put in clams, cover, and cook, stirring intermittently, until clams open, 5 to 7 minutes.
2. Use a slotted spoon to move clams to big container and cover to keep warm; discard any clams that refuse to open. Stir water and clam juice into wine and bring to simmer. Decrease heat to low, cover, and keep warm.
3. Heat remaining 2 tablespoons oil in a Dutch oven on moderate heat until it starts to shimmer. Put in leek, bell pepper, and ½ teaspoon salt and cook till they become tender, eight to ten minutes. Put in rice and remaining garlic and cook, stirring often, until grain edges begin to turn translucent, approximately three minutes.
4. Put in 2 cups warm broth and cook, stirring often, until almost fully absorbed, approximately five minutes. Carry on cooking rice, stirring often and adding warm broth, 1 cup at a time, every few minutes as liquid is absorbed, until rice is creamy and cooked through but still somewhat firm in center, 12 to 14 minutes.
5. Remove from the heat, mix in 1 cup warm broth and adjust consistency with extra broth as required (rice mixture should have thin but creamy consistency; you may have broth left over). Mix in parsley mixture and sprinkle with salt and pepper to taste.

Nestle clams into rice along with any accumulated juices, cover, and allow to sit until heated through, 5 to 7 minutes. Serve with lemon wedges.

Spanish Paella

Yield: 6 Servings

Ingredients:

- ⅓ cup dry white wine
- ½ cup frozen peas, thawed
- ½ teaspoon saffron threads, crumbled
- 1 (14.5-ounce) can diced tomatoes, drained, minced, and drained again
- 1 bay leaf
- 1 onion, chopped fine
- 1 pound boneless, skinless chicken thighs, trimmed and halved crosswise
- 1 pound extra-large shrimp (21 to 25 per pound), peeled and deveined
- 1 red bell pepper, stemmed, seeded, and cut into ½-inch-wide strips
- 12 mussels, scrubbed and debearded
- 2 cups Bomba rice
- 2 tablespoons extra-virgin olive oil, plus extra as required
- 2 teaspoons chopped fresh parsley
- 3 cups chicken broth
- 8 garlic cloves, minced
- 8 ounces Spanish-style chorizo sausage, sliced on bias ½ inch thick
- Lemon wedges
- Salt and pepper

Directions:

1. Place oven rack to lower-middle position and pre-heat your oven to 350 degrees. Toss shrimp with 1 tablespoon oil, 1 teaspoon garlic, ¼ teaspoon salt, and ¼ teaspoon pepper in a container until evenly coated. Cover and put in the fridge until needed. Pat chicken dry using paper towels and sprinkle with salt and pepper.
2. Heat 2 teaspoons oil in a Dutch oven on moderate to high heat until it starts to shimmer. Put in bell pepper and cook, stirring intermittently, until skin begins to blister and turn spotty black, about 4 minutes; move to a container.
3. Heat remaining 1 teaspoon oil in now-empty pot until it starts to shimmer. Put in chicken in one layer and cook, without moving, until browned, approximately three minutes. Turn pieces and cook until browned on second side, approximately three minutes; move to different container. Decrease heat to medium and put in chorizo to now-empty pot. Cook, stirring often, until deeply browned and fat begins to render, approximately five minutes; move to a container with chicken.
4. Put in extra oil to fat left in pot to equal 2 tablespoons and heat on moderate heat until it starts to shimmer. Put in onion and cook till they become tender, approximately three minutes. Mix in remaining garlic and cook until aromatic, about 1 minute. Mix in tomatoes and cook until mixture begins to darken and thicken slightly, approximately three minutes. Mix in rice and cook until grains are well coated with tomato mixture, approximately two minutes.
5. Mix in broth, wine, saffron, bay leaf, and ½ teaspoon salt. Return chicken and chorizo to pot, increase heat to medium-high, and bring to boil, stirring intermittently. Cover, move pot to oven, and bake until almost all liquid is absorbed, fifteen to twenty minutes.
6. Remove pot from oven. Scatter shrimp and mussels evenly over rice and push hinge side of mussels into rice so they stand up. Cover, return pot to oven, and bake until shrimp are opaque throughout and mussels have opened, 10 to fifteen minutes.
7. For optional socarrat, move pot to stovetop and remove lid. Cook on moderate to high heat for approximately five minutes,

    rotating pot as required, until bottom layer of rice is thoroughly browned and crisp.

8. Discard any mussels that refuse to open and bay leaf, if it can be easily removed. Arrange bell pepper strips in pinwheel pattern over rice and drizzle peas over top. Cover and let paella sit for about five minutes. Sprinkle with parsley and serve with lemon wedges.

Spanish Style Brown Rice

Yield: 6 Servings

Ⓥ *This is a Vegetarian Recipe* Ⓥ

Ingredients:

- ¼ cup minced fresh cilantro
- 1 cup long-grain brown rice, rinsed
- 1 onion, chopped fine
- 1 tablespoon lime juice
- 12 ounces grape tomatoes, quartered
- 2 (15-ounce) cans chickpeas, rinsed
- 2 red bell peppers, stemmed, seeded, and chopped fine
- 3¼ cups chicken or vegetable broth
- 4 garlic cloves, minced
- 4 teaspoons extra-virgin olive oil
- 5 scallions, sliced thin
- Pinch cayenne pepper
- Pinch saffron threads, crumbled
- Salt and pepper

Directions:

1. Mix tomatoes, scallions, cilantro, 2 teaspoons oil, and lime juice in a container. Sprinkle with salt and pepper to taste; set aside for serving.

2. Heat remaining 2 teaspoons oil in a big saucepan on moderate to high heat until it starts to shimmer. Put in bell peppers and onion and cook till they become tender and lightly browned, eight to ten minutes. Mix in rice, garlic, saffron, and cayenne and cook until aromatic, approximately half a minute.

3. Mix in broth and bring to simmer. Decrease heat to moderate to low, cover, and simmer, stirring intermittently, for 25 minutes.

4. Mix in chickpeas, cover, and simmer until rice becomes soft and broth is almost completely absorbed, about half an hour. Sprinkle with salt and pepper to taste. Serve, topping individual portions with tomato mixture.

Spiced Basmati Rice Mix

Yield: 8 to 10 Servings

Ⓥ *This is a Vegetarian Recipe* Ⓥ

Ingredients:

- ¼ cup extra-virgin olive oil
- ½ cup pomegranate seeds
- ½ teaspoon ground cinnamon
- ½ teaspoon ground cumin
- ½ teaspoon ground turmeric
- 1 head cauliflower (2 pounds), cored and cut into ¾-inch florets
- 1 onion, chopped coarse
- 1½ cups basmati rice, rinsed
- 2 tablespoons chopped fresh cilantro
- 2 tablespoons chopped fresh mint
- 2¼ cups water
- 4 garlic cloves, minced
- Salt and pepper

Directions:

1. Place oven rack on the lowest position and pre-heat your oven to 475 degrees. Toss cauliflower with 2 tablespoons oil, ½ teaspoon salt, ½ teaspoon pepper, and ¼ teaspoon cumin. Arrange cauliflower in one layer in rimmed baking sheet and roast until just tender, 10 to fifteen minutes; set aside.
2. Heat remaining 2 tablespoons oil in a big saucepan on moderate heat until it starts to shimmer. Put in onion and ¼ teaspoon salt and cook till they become tender and lightly browned, 5 to 7 minutes. Put in rice, garlic, cinnamon, turmeric, and remaining ¼ teaspoon cumin and cook, stirring often, until grain edges begin to turn translucent, approximately three minutes.
3. Mix in water and bring to simmer. Decrease heat to low, cover, and simmer gently until rice becomes soft and water is absorbed, 16 to 18 minutes.
4. Remove from the heat, lay clean dish towel underneath lid and let pilaf sit for about ten minutes. Put in roasted cauliflower to pilaf and fluff gently with fork to combine. Sprinkle with salt and pepper to taste. Move to serving platter and drizzle with pomegranate seeds, cilantro, and mint. Serve.

Tangy Rice Salad

Yield: 4 to 6 Servings

ⓋⓋ *This is a Vegetarian Recipe* Ⓥ

Ingredients:

- ⅓ cup large pitted brine-cured green olives, chopped
- ⅓ cup slivered almonds, toasted
- 1 small garlic clove, minced
- 1½ cups basmati rice

- 2 oranges, plus ¼ teaspoon grated orange zest plus 1 tablespoon juice
- 2 tablespoons extra-virgin olive oil
- 2 tablespoons minced fresh oregano
- 2 teaspoons sherry vinegar
- Salt and pepper

Directions:

1. Bring 4 quarts water to boil in a Dutch oven. In the meantime, toast rice in 12-inch frying pan on moderate heat until faintly aromatic and some grains turn opaque, five to ten minutes. Put in rice and 1½ teaspoons salt to boiling water and cook, stirring intermittently, until rice becomes soft but not soft, about fifteen minutes. Drain rice, spread onto rimmed baking sheet, and allow to cool completely, about fifteen minutes.
2. Cut away peel and pith from oranges. Holding fruit over bowl, use paring knife to slice between membranes to release segments. Beat oil, vinegar, garlic, orange zest and juice, 1 teaspoon salt, and ½ teaspoon pepper together in a big container. Put in rice, orange segments, olives, almonds, and oregano, gently toss to combine, and allow to sit for 20 minutes. Serve.

Tangy Wheat Berry Salad

Yield: 4 to 6 Servings

Ⓥ This is a Vegetarian Recipe Ⓥ

Ingredients:

- ⅛ teaspoon grated orange zest
- 1 garlic clove, minced
- 1 orange
- 1 small shallot, minced
- 1 tablespoon minced fresh tarragon

- 1½ cups wheat berries
- 1½ tablespoons Dijon mustard
- 1½ teaspoons honey
- 2 tablespoons extra-virgin olive oil
- 3 carrots, peeled and shredded
- 3 tablespoons red wine vinegar
- Salt and pepper

Directions:

1. Bring 4 quarts water to boil in a Dutch oven. Put in wheat berries and 1½ teaspoons salt, return to boil, and cook until soft but still chewy, 60 to 70 minutes. Drain wheat berries, spread in rimmed baking sheet, and allow to cool completely, about fifteen minutes.
2. Cut away peel and pith from orange. Quarter orange, then slice crosswise into ¼-inch-thick pieces. Beat vinegar, mustard, shallot, garlic, orange zest, honey, and ¼ teaspoon salt together in a big container until combined. Whisking continuously, slowly drizzle in oil. Put in wheat berries, carrots, tarragon, and orange pieces and gently toss to coat. Sprinkle with salt and pepper to taste. Serve.

Ultimate Barley Mix

Yield: 4 Servings

Ⓥ *This is a Vegetarian Recipe* Ⓥ

Ingredients:

- ½ cup black lentils, picked over and rinsed
- ½ cup Tahini-Yogurt Sauce
- ½ ounce dried porcini mushrooms, rinsed
- ¾ teaspoon ground coriander
- 1 cup pearl barley
- 1 onion, chopped fine

- 2 large portobello mushroom caps, cut into 1-inch pieces
- 2 tablespoons chopped fresh dill
- 2 tablespoons extra-virgin olive oil
- 3 (2-inch) strips lemon zest, sliced thin along the length
- Salt and pepper

Directions:

1. Microwave 1½ cups water and porcini mushrooms in covered bowl until steaming, about 1 minute. Allow to sit till they become tender, approximately five minutes. Drain mushrooms using a fine-mesh strainer lined with coffee filter, reserving soaking liquid, and chop mushrooms.
2. Bring 4 quarts water to boil in a Dutch oven. Put in barley, lentils, and 1 tablespoon salt, return to boil, and cook until tender, 20 to 40 minutes. Drain barley and lentils, return to now-empty pot, and cover to keep warm.
3. In the meantime, heat oil in 12-inch non-stick frying pan on moderate heat until it starts to shimmer. Put in onion and cook till they become tender, approximately five minutes. Mix in portobello mushrooms, cover, and cook until portobellos have released their liquid and begin to brown, about 4 minutes.
4. Uncover, mix in lemon zest, coriander, ½ teaspoon salt, and ¼ teaspoon pepper, and cook until aromatic, approximately half a minute. Mix in porcini and porcini soaking liquid, bring to boil, and cook, stirring intermittently, until liquid becomes thick slightly and reduced to ½ cup, approximately five minutes. Stir mushroom mixture and dill into barley-lentil mixture and sprinkle with salt and pepper to taste. Serve, drizzling individual portions with Tahini-Yogurt Sauce.

Vibrant Egyptian Barley Salad

Yield: 6 to 8 Servings

Ⓥ *This is a Vegetarian Recipe* Ⓥ

Ingredients:

- ¼ cup shelled pistachios, toasted and chopped coarse
- ¼ teaspoon ground cumin
- ⅓ cup golden raisins
- ½ cup coarsely chopped cilantro
- ½ cup pomegranate seeds
- ½ teaspoon ground cinnamon
- 1½ cups pearl barley
- 2 tablespoons pomegranate molasses
- 3 ounces feta cheese, cut into ½-inch cubes (¾ cup)
- 3 tablespoons extra-virgin olive oil, plus extra for serving
- 6 scallions, green parts only, sliced thin
- Salt and pepper

Directions:

1. Bring 4 quarts water to boil in a Dutch oven. Put in barley and 1 tablespoon salt, return to boil, and cook until tender, 20 to 40 minutes. Drain barley, spread onto rimmed baking sheet, and allow to cool completely, about fifteen minutes.
2. Beat oil, molasses, cinnamon, cumin, and ½ teaspoon salt together in a big container. Put in barley, raisins, cilantro, and pistachios and gently toss to combine. Sprinkle with salt and pepper to taste. Lay out barley salad uniformly serving platter and arrange feta, scallions, and pomegranate seeds in separate diagonal rows on top. Sprinkle with extra oil and serve.

Vibrant Spanish Grilled Paella

Yield: 8 Servings

Ingredients:

- ½ cup jarred roasted red peppers, rinsed, patted dry, and chopped fine
- ⅔ cup dry sherry

- 1 (8-ounce) bottle clam juice
- 1 cup frozen peas, thawed
- 1 onion, chopped fine
- 1 pound littleneck clams, scrubbed
- 1½ pounds boneless, skinless chicken thighs, trimmed and halved crosswise
- 1¾ teaspoons hot smoked paprika
- 12 ounces jumbo shrimp (16 to 20 per pound), peeled and deveined
- 3 cups Bomba rice
- 3 tablespoons tomato paste
- 4½ cups chicken broth
- 5 tablespoons extra-virgin olive oil
- 6 garlic cloves, minced
- 8 ounces Spanish-style chorizo sausage, cut into ½-inch pieces
- Lemon wedges
- Pinch saffron threads, crumbled (optional)
- Salt and pepper

Directions:

1. Pat chicken dry using paper towels and season both sides with 1 teaspoon salt and 1 teaspoon pepper. Toss shrimp with 1½ teaspoons oil, ½ teaspoon garlic, ¼ teaspoon paprika, and ¼ teaspoon salt in a container until evenly coated. Set aside.

2. Heat 1½ teaspoons oil in moderate-sized saucepan on moderate heat until it starts to shimmer. Put in remaining garlic and cook, stirring continuously, until garlic sticks to bottom of saucepan and begins to brown, about 1 minute. Put in tomato paste and remaining 1½ teaspoons paprika and continue to cook, stirring continuously, until dark brown bits form on bottom of saucepan, about 1 minute. Mix in 4 cups broth, sherry, clam juice, and saffron, if using. Increase heat to high and bring to boil. Remove saucepan from heat and set aside.

3. FOR A CHARCOAL GRILL: Open bottom vent fully. Light large chimney starter mounded with charcoal briquettes (7 quarts). When top coals are partially covered with ash, pour uniformly

over grill. Using tongs, arrange 20 unlit briquettes evenly over coals. Set cooking grate in place, cover, and open lid vent fully. Heat grill until hot, approximately five minutes.

4. FOR A GAS GRILL: Turn all burners to high, cover, and heat grill until hot, about fifteen minutes. Leave all burners on high.

5. Clean and oil cooking grate. Place chicken on grill and cook until both sides are lightly browned, 5 to 7 minutes; move chicken to plate and clean cooking grate.

6. Place roasting pan on grill (turning burners to medium-high if using gas) and put in remaining ¼ cup oil. When oil begins to shimmer, put in onion, red peppers, and ½ teaspoon salt. Cook, stirring often, until onion begins to brown, four to eight minutes. Mix in rice (turning burners to medium if using gas) until grains are well coated with oil.

7. Place the chicken around the perimeter of the pan. Pour chicken broth mixture and any accumulated chicken juices over rice. Level the rice into a uniform layer, making sure nothing sticks to sides of pan and no rice rests atop chicken. When liquid starts to mildly simmer, place shrimp in center of pan in one layer. Arrange clams in center of pan, evenly dispersing with shrimp and pushing hinge side of clams into rice slightly so they stand up. Distribute chorizo uniformly on the surface of rice. Cook, moving and rotating pan to maintain mild simmer across entire surface of pan, until rice is almost cooked through, about 12 to 18 minutes. Regulate the gas heat to maintain the simmer if you're using gas.

8. Sprinkle peas evenly over paella, cover grill, and cook until liquid is fully absorbed and rice on bottom of pan sizzles, five to ten minutes. Carry on cooking, uncovered, checking often, until an evenly golden-brown crust is achieved on the bottom of pan, about eight to fifteen minutes longer. (Rotate and slide pan around grill as necessary to ensure even crust formation.) Remove from grill, cover with aluminium foil, and allow to sit for about ten minutes. Serve with lemon wedges.

Wheat Berry Mix

Yield: 4 to 6 Servings

(V) This is a Vegetarian Recipe (V)

Ingredients:

- 1 garlic clove, minced
- 1 red bell pepper, stemmed, seeded, and cut into ½-inch pieces
- 1 red onion, chopped
- 1 tablespoon grated lemon zest
- 1 tablespoon minced fresh oregano or 1½ teaspoons dried
- 1 zucchini, cut into ½-inch pieces
- 1½ cups wheat berries
- 2 tablespoons extra-virgin olive oil
- 3 tablespoons red wine vinegar
- Salt and pepper

Directions:

1. Bring 4 quarts water to boil in a Dutch oven. Put in wheat berries and 1½ teaspoons salt, return to boil, and cook until soft but still chewy, 60 to 70 minutes.
2. In the meantime, beat 1 tablespoon oil, vinegar, garlic, lemon zest, and oregano together in a big container. Drain wheat berries, put in to a container with dressing, and toss gently to coat.
3. Heat 2 teaspoons oil in 12-inch non-stick frying pan on moderate to high heat until just smoking. Put in zucchini and ¼ teaspoon salt and cook, stirring intermittently, until deep golden brown and starting to char in spots, six to eight minutes; move to a container with wheat berries.
4. Return now-empty frying pan to medium-high heat and put in remaining 1 teaspoon oil, onion, bell pepper, and ¼ teaspoon salt. Cook, stirring intermittently, until onion is charred at edges and pepper skin is charred and blistered, eight to ten minutes. Put in wheat berry–zucchini mixture and cook, stirring often,

until heated through, approximately two minutes. Sprinkle with salt and pepper to taste. Serve.

Pasta and Couscous

When you think Pasta, Italy is the first thing that comes to mind. However, pasta is highly popular is other Mediterranean countries too. Various versions of pasta are a staple all across the Mediterranean, and we will take a look at a few of the best recipes in this section.

Pasta Sauces

The sauce is the life of the pasta!

Classic Marinara Sauce

Ⓥ This is a Vegetarian Recipe Ⓥ

This sauce works well with any type of pasta. If you prefer a chunkier sauce, give it just three or four pulses in the food processor in step 4.

Ingredients:

- ⅓ cup dry red wine
- 1 onion, chopped fine
- 2 (28-ounce) cans whole peeled tomatoes
- 2 garlic cloves, minced
- 2 teaspoons minced fresh oregano or ½ teaspoon dried
- 3 tablespoons chopped fresh basil
- 3 tablespoons extra-virgin olive oil
- Salt and pepper
- Sugar

Directions:

1. Drain tomatoes using a fine-mesh strainer set over big container. Using hands, open tomatoes and remove and discard seeds and fibrous cores; let tomatoes drain, approximately five minutes. Reserve ¾ cup tomatoes separately. Reserve 2½ cups drained tomato juice; discard extra juice.
2. Heat 2 tablespoons oil in 12-inch frying pan on moderate heat until it starts to shimmer. Put in onion and cook till they become tender and lightly browned, 5 to 7 minutes. Mix in garlic and oregano and cook until aromatic, approximately half a minute. Mix in remaining drained tomatoes and increase heat to medium-high. Cook, stirring frequently, until liquid has evaporated and tomatoes begin to brown and stick to pan, 10 to 12 minutes.
3. Mix in wine and cook until thick and syrupy, about 1 minute. Mix in reserved tomato juice, scraping up any browned bits. Bring to simmer and cook, stirring intermittently, until sauce is thickened, eight to ten minutes.
4. Move sauce to your food processor, put in reserved ¾ cup tomatoes, and pulse until slightly chunky, approximately 8 pulses. Return sauce to now-empty skillet, mix in basil and remaining 1 tablespoon oil, and season with salt, pepper, and sugar to taste. While you toss sauce with cooked pasta, gradually pour in some pasta cooking water as required to regulate consistency.

Fresh & Raw Tomato Sauce

⚡This recipe can be made quickly ⚡

Ⓥ This is a Vegetarian Recipe Ⓥ

Make sure the tomatoes are in season, and ripe.

Ingredients:

- ¼ cup extra-virgin olive oil
- 1 garlic clove, minced

- 1 shallot, minced
- 2 pounds very ripe tomatoes, cored and cut into ½-inch pieces
- 2 teaspoons lemon juice, plus extra as required
- 3 tablespoons chopped fresh basil
- Salt and pepper
- Sugar

Directions:

1. Stir oil, lemon juice, shallot, garlic, 1 teaspoon salt, ¼ teaspoon pepper, and pinch sugar together in a big container. Mix in tomatoes and allow to marinate until very soft and flavorful, approximately half an hour.
2. Before you serve, mix in basil and season with salt, pepper, sugar, and extra lemon juice to taste. While you toss sauce with cooked pasta, gradually pour in some pasta cooking water as required to regulate consistency.

Quick Tomato Sauce

✔ This recipe can be made quickly ✔

Ⓥ *This is a Vegetarian Recipe* Ⓥ

This sauce works well with any type of pasta.

Ingredients:

- ¼ teaspoon sugar
- 1 (14.5-ounce) can diced tomatoes
- 1 (28-ounce) can crushed tomatoes
- 3 garlic cloves, minced
- 3 tablespoons chopped fresh basil
- 3 tablespoons extra-virgin olive oil
- Salt and pepper

Directions:

1. Cook oil and garlic in moderate-sized saucepan on moderate heat, stirring frequently, until aromatic but not browned, approximately two minutes. Mix in tomatoes and their juice. Bring to simmer and cook until slightly thickened, fifteen to twenty minutes. Remove from the heat, mix in basil and sugar.
2. Sprinkle with salt and pepper to taste. While you toss sauce with cooked pasta, gradually pour in some pasta cooking water as required to regulate consistency.

Pesto Sauces

Pesto is a versatile Italian condiment that goes great with pasta, and can also be used for garnishing your favourite recipes!

Classic Basil Pesto

Yield: ¾ cup

⚡This recipe can be made quickly⚡

Ⓥ *This is a Vegetarian Recipe* Ⓥ

Ingredients:

- ¼ cup grated Parmesan cheese
- ¼ cup pine nuts, toasted
- 2 cups fresh basil leaves, lightly bruised
- 2 tablespoons fresh parsley leaves (optional)
- 3 garlic cloves, toasted and minced
- 7 tablespoons extra-virgin olive oil

Directions:

1. Process all ingredients except oil and cheese using a food processor until smooth, scraping down bowl as required. While your food processor runs slowly put in oil until incorporated.

2. Move pesto to a container, mix in cheese, and sprinkle with salt and pepper to taste. When tossing pesto with cooked pasta, put in some of pasta cooking water as required (up to ½ cup) to loosen consistency of pesto.
3. Pesto will keep safely in a fridge for maximum 3 days or frozen for maximum 3 months. To stop browning, press plastic wrap flush to surface, or top with thin layer of olive oil.

Green Olive and Orange Pesto

Yield: 1½ cups

✦This recipe can be made quickly ✦

Ⓥ *This is a Vegetarian Recipe* Ⓥ

Ingredients:

- ½ cup extra-virgin olive oil
- ½ cup pitted green olives
- ½ cup slivered almonds, toasted
- ½ teaspoon grated orange zest plus 2 tablespoons juice
- 1½ cups fresh parsley leaves
- 1½ ounces Parmesan cheese, grated (¾ cup)
- 2 garlic cloves, toasted and minced

Directions:

1. Process all ingredients except oil and cheese using a food processor until smooth, scraping down bowl as required. While your food processor runs slowly put in oil until incorporated.
2. Move pesto to a container, mix in cheese, and sprinkle with salt and pepper to taste. When tossing pesto with cooked pasta, put in some of pasta cooking water as required (up to ½ cup) to loosen consistency of pesto.

3. Pesto will keep safely in a fridge for maximum 3 days or frozen for maximum 3 months. To stop browning, press plastic wrap flush to surface, or top with thin layer of olive oil.

Roasted Red Pepper Pesto

Yield: 1½ cups

✄ This recipe can be made quickly ✄

Ⓥ *This is a Vegetarian Recipe* Ⓥ

Ingredients:

- ¼ cup fresh parsley leaves
- ¼ cup grated Parmesan cheese
- ½ cup extra-virgin olive oil
- 1 shallot, chopped
- 1 tablespoon fresh thyme leaves
- 2 roasted red bell peppers, peeled and chopped (1 cup)
- 3 garlic cloves, toasted and minced

Directions:

1. Process all ingredients except oil and cheese using a food processor until smooth, scraping down bowl as required. While your food processor runs slowly put in oil until incorporated.
2. Move pesto to a container, mix in cheese, and sprinkle with salt and pepper to taste. When tossing pesto with cooked pasta, put in some of pasta cooking water as required (up to ½ cup) to loosen consistency of pesto.
3. Pesto will keep safely in a fridge for maximum 3 days or frozen for maximum 3 months. To stop browning, press plastic wrap flush to surface, or top with thin layer of olive oil.

Tomato and Almond Pesto

Yield: 1½ cups

⚡This recipe can be made quickly⚡

Ⓥ This is a Vegetarian Recipe Ⓥ

Ingredients:

- ¼ cup slivered almonds, toasted
- ⅓ cup extra-virgin olive oil
- ½ cup fresh basil leaves
- 1 garlic clove, toasted and minced
- 1 ounce Parmesan cheese, grated (½ cup)
- 1 small pepperoncini, stemmed, seeded, and minced
- 12 ounces cherry or grape tomatoes
- Pinch red pepper flakes (optional)

Directions:

1. Process all ingredients except oil and cheese using a food processor until smooth, scraping down bowl as required. While your food processor runs slowly put in oil until incorporated.
2. Move pesto to a container, mix in cheese, and sprinkle with salt and pepper to taste. When tossing pesto with cooked pasta, put in some of pasta cooking water as required (up to ½ cup) to loosen consistency of pesto.
3. Pesto will keep safely in a fridge for maximum 3 days or frozen for maximum 3 months. To stop browning, press plastic wrap flush to surface, or top with thin layer of olive oil.

Pasta

And now to the Pasta recipes! You don't have to stick to the sauce suggestion given in the recipe. Feel free to experiment with one of the sauces you've already seen above! This section covers all the popular versions of pasta in the Mediterranean.

Briny Italian Spaghetti

Yield: 6 Servings

⚡ This recipe can be made quickly ⚡

Ingredients:

- ½ cup dry white wine
- ½ teaspoon red pepper flakes
- 1 pound mussels, scrubbed and debearded
- 1 pound spaghetti or linguine
- 1 tablespoon extra-virgin olive oil
- 1 teaspoon grated lemon zest plus 2 tablespoons juice
- 2 garlic cloves, minced
- 2 tablespoons minced fresh parsley
- Salt and pepper

Directions:

1. Bring mussels and wine to boil in 12-inch straight-sided sauté pan, cover, and cook, shaking pan occasionally, until mussels open, approximately five minutes. As mussels open, remove them using a slotted spoon and move to a container. Discard any mussels that refuse to open. (If desired, remove mussels from shells.) Drain steaming liquid through fine-mesh strainer lined with coffee filter into a container, avoiding any gritty sediment that has settled on bottom of pan. Wipe frying pan clean using paper towels.

2. Cook oil, garlic, and pepper flakes in now-empty pan on moderate heat, stirring often, until garlic turns golden but not brown, approximately three minutes. Mix in reserved mussel steaming liquid and lemon zest and juice, bring to simmer, and

cook until flavours blend, about 4 minutes. Mix in mussels, cover, and cook until heated through, approximately two minutes.

3. In the meantime, bring 4 quarts water to boil in large pot. Put in pasta and 1 tablespoon salt and cook, stirring frequently, until al dente. Reserve ½ cup cooking water, then drain pasta and return it to pot. Put in sauce and parsley and toss to combine. Sprinkle with salt and pepper to taste and regulate consistency with reserved cooking water as required. Serve.

Cheesy Penne with Roasted Cherry Tomatoes

Yield: 6 Servings

Ⓥ This is a Vegetarian Recipe Ⓥ

Ingredients:

- ¼ cup extra-virgin olive oil
- ¼ teaspoon red pepper flakes
- 1 pound penne
- 1 shallot, sliced thin
- 1 tablespoon sherry or red wine vinegar
- 1½ teaspoons sugar, or to taste
- 2 pounds cherry tomatoes, halved
- 3 large garlic cloves, sliced thin
- 4 ounces (4 cups) baby arugula
- 4 ounces goat cheese, crumbled (1 cup)
- Salt and pepper

Directions:

1. Place the oven rack in the centre of the oven and pre-heat your oven to 350 degrees. Toss shallot with 1 teaspoon oil in a container. In a different container, gently toss tomatoes with remaining oil, garlic, vinegar, sugar, ½ teaspoon salt, ¼ teaspoon

pepper, and pepper flakes. Lay out tomato mixture in a uniform layer in rimmed baking sheet, scatter shallot over tomatoes, and roast until edges of shallot begin to brown and tomato skins are slightly shriveled, 35 to 40 minutes. (Do not stir tomatoes during roasting.) Allow it to cool for 5 to 10 minutes.

2. In the meantime, bring 4 quarts water to boil in large pot. Put in pasta and 1 tablespoon salt and cook, stirring frequently, until al dente. Reserve ½ cup cooking water, then drain pasta and return it to pot. Put in arugula to pasta and toss until wilted. Using rubber spatula, scrape tomato mixture onto pasta and toss to combine. Sprinkle with salt and pepper to taste and regulate consistency with reserved cooking water as required. Serve, passing goat cheese separately.

Classic Clammed Italian Spaghetti

Yield: 6 Servings

Ingredients:

- ⅛ teaspoon red pepper flakes
- ⅓ cup chopped fresh mint or parsley
- ½ cup dry white wine
- 1 pound spaghetti or linguine
- 1 shallot, sliced thin
- 12 cloves garlic, peeled (8 smashed, 4 minced)
- 2 tablespoons tomato paste
- 2 teaspoons minced fresh thyme or ½ teaspoon dried
- 3 pounds ripe tomatoes, cored and halved
- 3 tablespoons extra-virgin olive oil, plus extra for serving
- 4 pounds littleneck clams, scrubbed
- Salt and pepper

Directions:

1. Place the oven rack in the centre of the oven and pre-heat your oven to 475 degrees. Mix tomato paste, 1 tablespoon oil, thyme,

¼ teaspoon salt, and ¼ teaspoon pepper in a big container. Put in tomatoes and smashed garlic and gently toss to coat. Place 4-inch square of aluminium foil in center of wire rack set in rimmed baking sheet lined with aluminium foil. Place smashed garlic cloves on foil and arrange tomatoes, cut side down, around garlic. Roast until tomatoes are soft and skins are well charred, 45 to 55 minutes.

2. Heat remaining 2 tablespoons oil in a Dutch oven on moderate heat until it starts to shimmer. Put in shallot, pepper flakes, and minced garlic and cook until aromatic, about 1 minute. Mix in wine and cook until almost completely evaporated, about 1 minute. Mix in roasted tomatoes and garlic and bring to boil. Put in clams, cover, and cook, shaking pot occasionally, until clams open, about four to eight minutes. As clams open, remove them using a slotted spoon and move to a container. Discard any clams that refuse to open. (If desired, remove clams from shells.)

3. In the meantime, bring 4 quarts water to boil in large pot. Put in pasta and 1 tablespoon salt and cook, stirring frequently, until al dente. Reserve ½ cup cooking water, then drain pasta and put in to pot with sauce. Put in mint and toss to combine. Sprinkle with salt and pepper to taste and regulate consistency with reserved cooking water as required. Move pasta to serving bowl, top with clams, and drizzle with extra oil. Serve.

Classic Italian Linguine ai Frutti di Mare

Yield: 6 Servings

Ingredients:

- ⅛ teaspoon red pepper flakes
- ⅛ teaspoon saffron threads, crumbled
- ⅓ cup minced fresh parsley
- 1 (28-ounce) can whole peeled tomatoes, drained
- 1 (8-ounce) bottle clam juice
- 1 anchovy fillet, rinsed and minced

- 1 cup dry white wine
- 1 cup Lemon-Chili Bread Crumbs
- 1 pound linguine
- 2 shallots, sliced thin
- 2 tablespoons tomato paste
- 3 tablespoons extra-virgin olive oil, plus extra for serving
- 6 garlic cloves, sliced thin
- 8 ounces large sea scallops, tendons removed
- 8 ounces large shrimp (26 to 30 per pound), peeled and deveined, shells reserved
- 8 ounces mussels, scrubbed and debearded
- 8 ounces squid, bodies sliced crosswise into ¼-inch-thick rings, tentacles halved

Directions:

1. Heat 1 tablespoon oil in a Dutch oven on moderate heat until it starts to shimmer. Put in shrimp shells and cook, stirring often, until starting to turn spotty brown and pot starts to brown, 2 to 4 minutes. Put in wine and simmer, stirring intermittently, for about five minutes. Strain mixture through fine-mesh strainer into a container, pressing on solids to extract as much liquid as possible; discard solids.

2. Pulse tomatoes using a food processor until finely ground, approximately ten pulses. Heat remaining 2 tablespoons oil in now-empty pot on moderate heat until it starts to shimmer. Put in shallots and cook till they become tender and lightly browned, 2 to 3 minutes. Mix in garlic, tomato paste, anchovy, pepper flakes, and saffron and cook until aromatic, about 1 minute. Mix in wine mixture, scraping up any browned bits, and cook until nearly evaporated, approximately half a minute. Mix in tomatoes and clam juice, bring to simmer, and cook, stirring intermittently, until thickened and flavours blend, approximately twenty minutes.

3. Put in mussels, bring to boil, cover, and cook, shaking pot occasionally, until mussels open, 3 to 6 minutes. As mussels

open, remove them using a slotted spoon and move to a
container. Discard any mussels that refuse to open.

4. Reduce sauce to simmer, gently mix in scallops, and cook for 2
    minutes. Gently mix in shrimp and cook until just opaque
    throughout, approximately two minutes. Remove from the heat,
    mix in squid, cover, and allow to sit until just opaque and tender,
    1 to 2 minutes.

5. In the meantime, bring 4 quarts water to boil in large pot. Put in
    pasta and 1 tablespoon salt and cook, stirring frequently, until al
    dente. Reserve ½ cup cooking water, then drain pasta and put in
    to pot with sauce. Put in mussels and parsley and toss to
    combine. Sprinkle with salt and pepper to taste and regulate
    consistency with reserved cooking water as required. Serve,
    sprinkling individual portions with bread crumbs and drizzling
    with extra oil.

Classic Italian Spaghetti al Limone

Yield: 6 Servings

This recipe can be made quickly

V This is a Vegetarian Recipe V

Ingredients:

- ½ cup extra-virgin olive oil
- 1 pound spaghetti
- 1 small garlic clove, minced to paste
- 2 ounces Parmesan cheese, grated (1 cup)
- 2 teaspoons grated lemon zest plus ⅓ cup lemon juice (2 lemons)
- 6 tablespoons shredded fresh basil
- Salt and pepper

Directions:

1. Beat oil, lemon zest and juice, garlic, ½ teaspoon salt, and ¼ teaspoon pepper together in a small-sized container, then mix in Parmesan until thick and creamy.
2. In the meantime, bring 4 quarts water to boil in large pot. Put in pasta and 1 tablespoon salt and cook, stirring frequently, until al dente. Reserve ½ cup cooking water, then drain pasta and return it to pot. Put in oil mixture and basil and toss to combine. Sprinkle with salt and pepper to taste and regulate consistency with reserved cooking water as required. Serve.

Colourful & Nutty Farfalle

Yield: 6 Servings

Ⓥ This is a Vegetarian Recipe Ⓥ

Ingredients:

- ¼ cup pine nuts, toasted
- ½ cup chopped fresh basil
- ½ teaspoon red pepper flakes
- 1 pound farfalle
- 12 ounces grape tomatoes, halved
- 2 pounds zucchini and/or summer squash, halved along the length and sliced ½ inch thick
- 2 tablespoons balsamic vinegar
- 3 garlic cloves, minced
- 5 tablespoons extra-virgin olive oil
- Grated Parmesan cheese
- Kosher salt and pepper

Directions:

1. Toss squash with 1 tablespoon salt and allow to drain using a colander for 30 minutes. Pat squash dry using paper towels and carefully wipe away any residual salt.

2. Heat 1 tablespoon oil in 12-inch non-stick frying pan on high heat until just smoking. Put in half of squash and cook, stirring intermittently, until golden brown and smildly charred, 5 to 7 minutes, reducing heat if frying pan begins to scorch; move to large plate. Repeat with 1 tablespoon oil and remaining squash; move to plate.

3. Heat 1 tablespoon oil in now-empty frying pan on moderate heat until it starts to shimmer. Put in garlic and pepper flakes and cook until aromatic, approximately half a minute. Mix in squash and cook until heated through, approximately half a minute.

4. In the meantime, bring 4 quarts water to boil in large pot. Put in pasta and 1 tablespoon salt and cook, stirring frequently, until al dente. Reserve ½ cup cooking water, then drain pasta and return it to pot. Put in squash mixture, tomatoes, basil, pine nuts, vinegar, and remaining 2 tablespoons oil and toss to combine. Sprinkle with salt and pepper to taste and regulate consistency with reserved cooking water as required. Serve with Parmesan.

Flavourful Italian Spaghetti Mix

Yield: 6 Servings

Ingredients:

- ¼–½ teaspoon red pepper flakes
- 1 (15-ounce) can cannellini beans, rinsed
- 1 cup Parmesan Bread Crumbs
- 1 onion, chopped fine
- 1 pound whole-wheat spaghetti
- 1 tablespoon extra-virgin olive oil
- 1½ cups chicken broth
- 1½ pounds kale or collard greens, stemmed and cut into 1-inch pieces
- 3 garlic cloves, minced
- 3 ounces pancetta, cut into ½-inch pieces
- 4 ounces fontina cheese, shredded (1 cup)

- Salt and pepper

Directions:

1. Heat oil in 12-inch straight-sided sauté pan on moderate heat until it starts to shimmer. Put in pancetta and cook, stirring intermittently, until crisp, 5 to 7 minutes. Use a slotted spoon to move pancetta to paper towel–lined plate.

2. Put in onion to fat left in pan and cook on moderate heat till they become tender and lightly browned, 5 to 7 minutes. Mix in garlic and pepper flakes and cook until aromatic, approximately half a minute. Put in half of greens and cook, tossing occasionally, until starting to wilt, approximately two minutes. Put in remaining greens, broth, and ¾ teaspoon salt and bring to simmer. Decrease heat to medium, cover (pan will be very full), and cook, tossing occasionally, until greens are tender, about fifteen minutes (mixture will be somewhat soupy). Remove from the heat, mix in beans and pancetta.

3. In the meantime, bring 4 quarts water to boil in large pot. Put in pasta and 1 tablespoon salt and cook, stirring frequently, until just shy of al dente. Reserve ½ cup cooking water, then drain pasta and return it to pot. Put in greens mixture and cook on moderate heat, tossing to combine, until pasta absorbs most of liquid, approximately two minutes.

4. Remove from the heat, mix in fontina. Sprinkle with salt and pepper to taste and regulate consistency with reserved cooking water as required. Serve, sprinkling individual portions with bread crumbs.

Flavourful Italian Tagliatelle

Yield: 6 Servings

Ingredients:

- ⅛ teaspoon red pepper flakes
- ¼ cup extra-virgin olive oil, plus extra for serving

- ¼ cup minced fresh parsley
- ½ cup dry white wine
- 1 ounce Parmesan cheese, grated (½ cup), plus extra for serving
- 1 pound tagliatelle
- 1 recipe Parmesan Bread Crumbs
- 1 tablespoon minced fresh oregano or 1 teaspoon dried
- 1½ teaspoons grated lemon zest
- 2 anchovy fillets, rinsed, patted dry, and minced
- 4 cups jarred whole baby artichoke hearts packed in water
- 4 garlic cloves, minced
- Salt and pepper

Directions:

1. Cut leaves from artichoke hearts. Cut hearts in half and dry using paper towels. Place leaves in a container and cover with water. Let leaves sit for about fifteen minutes. Drain well.
2. Heat 1 tablespoon oil in 12-inch non-stick frying pan on moderate to high heat until it starts to shimmer. Put in artichoke hearts and ⅛ teaspoon salt and cook, stirring often, until spotty brown, seven to nine minutes. Mix in garlic, anchovies, oregano, and pepper flakes and cook, stirring continuously, until aromatic, approximately half a minute. Mix in wine and bring to simmer. Remove from the heat, mix in artichoke leaves.
3. In the meantime, bring 4 quarts water to boil in large pot. Put in pasta and 1 tablespoon salt and cook, stirring frequently, until al dente. Reserve 1½ cups cooking water, then drain pasta and return it to pot. Put in 1 cup reserved cooking water, artichoke mixture, Parmesan, parsley, lemon zest, and remaining 3 tablespoons oil and toss to combine. Sprinkle with salt and pepper to taste and regulate consistency with remaining ½ cup reserved cooking water as required. Serve, sprinkling individual portions with bread crumbs and extra Parmesan (recipe belo) and drizzling with extra oil.

Parmesan Bread Crumbs

Yield: 1 cup

✶ This recipe can be made quickly ✶

Ⓥ This is a Vegetarian Recipe Ⓥ

Ingredients:

- ¼ cup grated Parmesan cheese
- 2 slices hearty white sandwich bread
- 2 tablespoons extra-virgin olive oil
- Salt and pepper

Directions:

1. Pulse bread using a food processor until finely ground, 10 to 15 pulses. Heat oil in 12-inch non-stick frying pan on moderate heat until it starts to shimmer.
2. Put in bread crumbs and cook, stirring continuously, until crumbs begin to brown, 3 to 5 minutes. Put in Parmesan and continue to cook, stirring continuously, until crumbs start to look golden brown, 1 to 2 minutes. Move crumbs to a container and sprinkle with salt and pepper to taste. Serve.

Flavourful Toasted Orzo Mix

Yield: 6 to 8 Servings

Ⓥ This is a Vegetarian Recipe Ⓥ

Ingredients:

- ½ cup pitted kalamata olives, chopped
- ¾ cup dry white wine
- ¾ teaspoon fennel seeds
- 1 fennel bulb, stalks discarded, bulb halved, cored, and chopped fine

- 1 onion, chopped fine
- 1 teaspoon grated orange zest
- 1½ cups water
- 1½ ounces Parmesan cheese, grated (¾ cup)
- 2 cups chicken or vegetable broth
- 2 garlic cloves, minced
- 2 tablespoons extra-virgin olive oil
- 2⅔ cups orzo
- Pinch ground nutmeg
- Pinch red pepper flakes
- Salt and pepper

Directions:

1. Heat oil in 12-inch non-stick frying pan on moderate heat until it starts to shimmer. Put in fennel, onion, and ¾ teaspoon salt and cook till they become tender and lightly browned, 5 to 7 minutes. Mix in garlic, orange zest, fennel seeds, and pepper flakes and cook until aromatic, approximately half a minute. Put in orzo and cook, stirring often, until orzo is coated with oil and lightly browned, approximately five minutes.
2. Mix in broth, water, and wine and bring to boil. Cook, stirring intermittently, until all liquid has been absorbed and orzo is tender, 10 to fifteen minutes. Mix in olives, Parmesan, and nutmeg and sprinkle with salt and pepper to taste. Serve.

Greek Crunchy Orzo Salad

Yield: 4 to 6 Servings

Ⓥ *This is a Vegetarian Recipe* Ⓥ

Ingredients:

- ¼ cup extra-virgin olive oil, plus extra for serving
- ¼ cup pine nuts, toasted
- ½ cup chopped fresh basil

- ½ cup oil-packed sun-dried tomatoes, minced
- ½ cup pitted kalamata olives, halved
- 1 ounce Parmesan cheese, grated (½ cup)
- 1¼ cups orzo
- 2 garlic cloves, minced
- 2 ounces (2 cups) baby arugula, chopped
- 3 tablespoons balsamic vinegar
- Salt and pepper

Directions:

1. Bring 2 quarts water to boil in large pot. Put in orzo and 1½ teaspoons salt and cook, stirring frequently, until al dente. Drain orzo and move to rimmed baking sheet. Toss with 1 tablespoon oil and allow to cool completely, about fifteen minutes.
2. Beat remaining 3 tablespoons oil, vinegar, garlic, ½ teaspoon salt, and ½ teaspoon pepper together in a big container. Put in arugula, Parmesan, tomatoes, olives, basil, pine nuts, and orzo and gently toss to combine. Sprinkle with salt and pepper to taste. Let salad sit until flavours blend, approximately half an hour. Serve, drizzled with extra oil. (Salad will keep safely in a fridge for maximum 2 days.)

Greek Manestra

Yield: 6 Servings

Ⓥ This is a Vegetarian Recipe Ⓥ

Ingredients:

- 1 onion, chopped fine
- 1 ounce Parmesan cheese, grated (½ cup)
- 1 pound eggplant, cut into ½-inch pieces
- 1¼ cups chicken or vegetable broth
- 1¼ cups water
- 2 anchovy fillets, rinsed, patted dry, and minced

- 2 cups orzo
- 2 tablespoons capers, rinsed and minced
- 2 teaspoons tomato paste
- 3 garlic cloves, minced
- 3 ounces feta cheese, crumbled (¾ cup)
- 3 tablespoons extra-virgin olive oil, plus extra for serving
- 4 teaspoons minced fresh oregano or 1 teaspoon dried
- 4 tomatoes, cored and sliced ¼ inch thick
- Salt and pepper

Directions:

1. Place oven rack to upper-middle position and pre-heat your oven to 400 degrees. Line large plate using double layer of coffee filters and spray using vegetable oil spray. Toss eggplant with ½ teaspoon salt and spread uniformly coffee filters. Microwave eggplant, uncovered, until dry to touch and slightly shriveled, 7 to 10 minutes, tossing halfway through microwaving.
2. Toast orzo in 12-inch non-stick frying pan on moderate to high heat until lightly browned, 3 to 5 minutes; move to a container. Heat 1 tablespoon oil in now-empty frying pan on moderate to high heat until it starts to shimmer. Put in eggplant and cook, stirring intermittently, until well browned, 5 to 7 minutes; move to different container.
3. Heat remaining 2 tablespoons oil in again-empty frying pan on moderate heat until it starts to shimmer. Put in onion and cook till they become tender and lightly browned, 5 to 7 minutes. Mix in garlic, 1 tablespoon oregano, tomato paste, and anchovies and cook until aromatic, approximately half a minute. Remove from the heat, mix in orzo, eggplant, broth, water, Parmesan, capers, and ¼ teaspoon pepper. Move to greased 13 by 9-inch baking dish and spread into even layer.
4. Shingle tomatoes beautifully over top, then drizzle with ¼ teaspoon salt. Bake until all liquid has been absorbed and orzo is tender, 30 to 35 minutes. Allow it to cool for about five minutes. Sprinkle feta and remaining 1 teaspoon oregano over tomatoes and drizzle with extra oil. Serve.

Greek Spicy Orzo

Yield: 4 to 6 Servings

Ingredients:

- ⅛ teaspoon red pepper flakes
- ¼ cup chopped fresh mint
- ¼ cup plain whole-milk Greek yogurt
- ¼ teaspoon ground cinnamon
- ½ cup dry white wine
- 1 onion, chopped fine
- 1 red bell pepper, stemmed, seeded, and chopped fine
- 1 tablespoon extra-virgin olive oil
- 1 tablespoon tomato paste
- 1 teaspoon paprika
- 1½ cups orzo
- 1½ teaspoons grated lemon zest
- 2 garlic cloves, minced
- 2½ cups chicken broth
- 4 ounces loukaniko sausage, chopped fine
- Salt and pepper

Directions:

1. Toast orzo in 12-inch frying pan on moderate to high heat until lightly browned, 3 to 5 minutes; move to a container. Heat oil in now-empty frying pan on moderate heat until it starts to shimmer. Put in sausage and cook until browned and fat is rendered, four to eight minutes.

2. Mix in onion and bell pepper and cook till they become tender, 5 to 7 minutes. Mix in tomato paste, garlic, paprika, cinnamon, and pepper flakes and cook until aromatic, about 1 minute. Mix in wine, scraping up any browned bits. Mix in broth and orzo and bring to simmer. Decrease heat to low, cover, and simmer gently

until most of liquid is absorbed, about 10 minutes, stirring once halfway through simmering.

3. Uncover and continue to cook, stirring intermittently, until orzo is al dente and creamy, about 4 minutes. Remove from the heat, mix in yogurt and lemon zest. Sprinkle with salt and pepper to taste and regulate consistency with hot water as required. Sprinkle with mint and serve.

Green Penne and Fresh Tomato Sauce

Yield: 6 Servings

⚡This recipe can be made quickly ⚡

Ⓥ This is a Vegetarian Recipe Ⓥ

Ingredients:

- 1 pound penne
- 2 garlic cloves, minced
- 2 tablespoons chopped fresh mint or oregano
- 2 tablespoons lemon juice
- 3 pounds ripe tomatoes, cored, peeled, seeded, and cut into ½-inch pieces
- 3 tablespoons extra-virgin olive oil
- 4 ounces feta cheese, crumbled (1 cup)
- 5 ounces (5 cups) baby spinach
- Salt and pepper
- Sugar
- The success of this recipe depends on ripe, in-season tomatoes.

Directions:

1. Cook 2 tablespoons oil and garlic in 12-inch frying pan on moderate heat, stirring frequently, until garlic turns golden but not brown, approximately three minutes. Mix in tomatoes and cook until tomato pieces begin to lose their shape, approximately

eight minutes. Mix in spinach, 1 handful at a time, and cook until spinach is wilted and tomatoes have made chunky sauce, approximately two minutes.

2. In the meantime, bring 4 quarts water to boil in large pot. Put in pasta and 1 tablespoon salt and cook, stirring frequently, until al dente. Reserve ½ cup cooking water, then drain pasta and return it to pot.

3. Stir mint, lemon juice, ¼ teaspoon salt, and ⅛ teaspoon pepper into sauce and season with sugar to taste. Put in sauce and residual 1 tablespoon oil to pasta and toss to combine. Sprinkle with salt and pepper to taste and regulate consistency with reserved cooking water as required. Serve, passing feta separately.

Lemony Shrimp Orzo

Yield: 4 Servings

Ingredients:

- ½ cup pitted kalamata olives, chopped coarse
- 1 onion, chopped fine
- 1 tablespoon grated lemon zest plus 1 tablespoon juice
- 1½ pounds extra-large shrimp (21 to 25 per pound), peeled and deveined
- 2 cups chicken broth
- 2 cups orzo
- 2 cups water
- 2 garlic cloves, minced
- 2 ounces feta cheese, crumbled (½ cup)
- 2 tablespoons chopped fresh parsley
- 2 tablespoons extra-virgin olive oil, plus extra for serving
- Salt and pepper

Directions:

1. Mix lemon zest, ½ teaspoon salt, and ½ teaspoon pepper in medium bowl. Put in shrimp, toss to coat, put inside your fridge until ready to use.
2. Heat 1 tablespoon oil in 12-inch non-stick frying pan on moderate to high heat until just smoking. Put in onion and cook till they become tender, approximately five minutes. Mix in garlic and cook until aromatic, approximately half a minute. Put in orzo and cook, stirring often, until orzo is coated with oil and lightly browned, approximately five minutes. Mix in broth and water and bring to boil. Cook, stirring intermittently, until orzo is al dente, about 6 minutes. Mix in olives, ¼ cup feta, and lemon juice. Sprinkle with salt and pepper to taste.
3. Decrease heat to moderate to low, nestle shrimp into orzo, cover, and cook until shrimp are opaque throughout, approximately five minutes. Sprinkle with parsley and remaining ¼ cup feta and drizzle with extra oil. Serve.

Nutty Penne with Roasted Cherry Tomatoes

Yield: 6 Servings

Ⓥ *This is a Vegetarian Recipe* Ⓥ

Ingredients:

- ¼ cup capers, rinsed
- ¼ cup extra-virgin olive oil
- ¼ cup pine nuts, toasted
- ½ cup pitted kalamata olives, chopped
- ½ teaspoon red pepper flakes
- 1 pound penne
- 1½ teaspoons sugar, or to taste
- 2 pounds cherry tomatoes, halved
- 3 large garlic cloves, sliced thin

- 3 tablespoons chopped fresh oregano
- Grated Pecorino Romano cheese
- Salt and pepper

Directions:

1. Place the oven rack in the centre of the oven and pre-heat your oven to 350 degrees. Gently toss tomatoes with oil, capers, garlic, sugar, ½ teaspoon salt, pepper flakes, and ¼ teaspoon pepper in a container. Lay out tomato mixture in a uniform layer in rimmed baking sheet and roast until tomato skins are slightly shriveled, 35 to 40 minutes. (Do not stir tomatoes during roasting.) Allow it to cool for 5 to 10 minutes.
2. In the meantime, bring 4 quarts water to boil in large pot. Put in pasta and 1 tablespoon salt and cook, stirring frequently, until al dente. Reserve ½ cup cooking water, then drain pasta and return it to pot. Using rubber spatula, scrape tomato mixture onto pasta. Put in olives, pine nuts, and oregano and toss to combine. Sprinkle with salt and pepper to taste and regulate consistency with reserved cooking water as required. Serve with Pecorino Romano.

Penne with Cherry Tomato Sauce

Yield: 6 Servings

Ⓥ *This is a Vegetarian Recipe* Ⓥ

Ingredients:

- ¼ cup coarsely chopped fresh basil
- ¼ cup extra-virgin olive oil
- ¼ teaspoon red pepper flakes
- 1 pound penne
- 1 shallot, sliced thin
- 1 tablespoon balsamic vinegar
- 1½ teaspoons sugar, or to taste

- 2 pounds cherry tomatoes, halved
- 3 large garlic cloves, sliced thin
- Grated Parmesan cheese
- Salt and pepper

Directions:

1. Place the oven rack in the centre of the oven and pre-heat your oven to 350 degrees. Toss shallot with 1 teaspoon oil in a container. In a different container, gently toss tomatoes with remaining oil, garlic, vinegar, sugar, ½ teaspoon salt, ¼ teaspoon pepper, and pepper flakes. Lay out tomato mixture in a uniform layer in rimmed baking sheet, scatter shallot over tomatoes, and roast until edges of shallot begin to brown and tomato skins are slightly shriveled, 35 to 40 minutes. (Do not stir tomatoes during roasting.) Allow it to cool for 5 to 10 minutes.
2. In the meantime, bring 4 quarts water to boil in large pot. Put in pasta and 1 tablespoon salt and cook, stirring frequently, until al dente. Reserve ½ cup cooking water, then drain pasta and return it to pot. Using rubber spatula, scrape tomato mixture onto pasta. Put in basil and toss to combine. Sprinkle with salt and pepper to taste and regulate consistency with reserved cooking water as required. Serve with Parmesan.

Puglia-Style Orecchiette

Yield: 6 Servings

This recipe can be made quickly

Ⓥ This is a Vegetarian Recipe Ⓥ

Ingredients:

- ¼ cup extra-virgin olive oil
- ¼ teaspoon red pepper flakes
- ½ teaspoon fennel seeds, crushed

- 1 (15-ounce) can cannellini beans, rinsed
- 1 pound broccoli rabe, trimmed and cut into 1½-inch pieces
- 1 pound orecchiette
- 1 shallot, minced
- 1 teaspoon minced fresh oregano or ¼ teaspoon dried
- 2 ounces Parmesan or Asiago cheese, grated (1 cup)
- 6 garlic cloves, minced
- Salt and pepper

Directions:

1. Heat oil in 12-inch non-stick frying pan on moderate heat until it starts to shimmer. Put in shallot and cook till they become tender, approximately two minutes. Mix in garlic, oregano, fennel seeds, and pepper flakes and cook until aromatic, approximately half a minute. Mix in beans and cook until heated through, approximately two minutes; set aside.
2. In the meantime, bring 4 quarts water to boil in large pot. Put in broccoli rabe and 1 tablespoon salt and cook, stirring frequently, until crisp-tender, approximately two minutes. Use a slotted spoon to move broccoli rabe to frying pan with bean mixture.
3. Return water to boil, put in pasta, and cook, stirring frequently, until al dente. Reserve 1 cup cooking water, then drain pasta and return it to pot. Put in bean–broccoli rabe mixture, Parmesan, and ⅓ cup reserved cooking water and toss to combine. Sprinkle with salt and pepper to taste and regulate consistency with remaining ⅔ cup reserved cooking water as required. Serve.

Rustic Italian Whole-Wheat Spaghetti

Yield: 6 Servings

Ingredients:

- ¼ cup chopped fresh parsley

- ¼ cup dry white wine
- ¼ cup extra-virgin olive oil
- ¾ cup lentilles du Puy, picked over and rinsed
- 1 head escarole (1 pound), trimmed and sliced ½ inch thick
- 1 onion, chopped fine
- 1 pound whole-wheat spaghetti
- 1½ cups water
- 2 carrots, peeled, halved along the length, and sliced ¼ inch thick
- 2 cups chicken broth
- 2 garlic cloves, minced
- 4 ounces pancetta, cut into ¼-inch pieces
- Grated Parmesan cheese
- Salt and pepper

Directions:

1. Heat 2 tablespoons oil in a big saucepan on moderate heat until it starts to shimmer. Put in pancetta and cook, stirring intermittently, until starting to brown, 3 to 5 minutes. Put in onion and carrots and cook till they become tender, 5 to 7 minutes. Mix in garlic and cook until aromatic, approximately half a minute. Mix in lentils, broth, and water and bring to simmer. Decrease heat to moderate to low, cover, and simmer until lentils are fully cooked and tender, 30 to 40 minutes.
2. Mix in wine and simmer, uncovered, for 2 minutes. Mix in escarole, 1 handful at a time, and cook until completely wilted, approximately five minutes.
3. In the meantime, bring 4 quarts water to boil in large pot. Put in pasta and 1 tablespoon salt and cook, stirring frequently, until al dente. Reserve ¾ cup cooking water, then drain pasta and return it to pot. Put in ½ cup reserved cooking water, lentil mixture, parsley, and remaining 2 tablespoons oil and toss to combine. Sprinkle with salt and pepper to taste and regulate consistency with remaining ¼ cup reserved cooking water as required. Serve with Parmesan.

Spanish Toasted Shrimpy Pasta

Yield: 4 Servings

Ingredients:

- ¼ cup dry white wine
- ½ teaspoon anchovy paste
- 1 (14.5-ounce) can diced tomatoes, drained and chopped fine
- 1 bay leaf
- 1 cup chicken broth
- 1 onion, chopped fine
- 1 tablespoon chopped fresh parsley
- 1 teaspoon paprika
- 1 teaspoon smoked paprika
- 1½ pounds extra-large shrimp (21 to 25 per pound), peeled and deveined, shells reserved
- 2¾ cups water
- 3 garlic cloves, minced
- 3 tablespoons plus 2 teaspoons extra-virgin olive oil
- 8 ounces vermicelli pasta or thin spaghetti, broken into 1- to 2-inch lengths
- Lemon wedges
- Salt and pepper

Directions:

1. Mix 1 tablespoon oil, 1 teaspoon garlic, ¼ teaspoon salt, and ⅛ teaspoon pepper in medium bowl. Put in shrimp, toss to coat, put inside your fridge until ready to use.
2. Place reserved shrimp shells, water, broth, and bay leaf in medium bowl. Cover and microwave until liquid is hot and shells have turned pink, about 6 minutes. Set aside until ready to use.
3. Toss pasta with 2 teaspoons oil in broiler-safe 12-inch frying pan until evenly coated. Toast pasta on moderate to high heat, stirring often, until browned and nutty in aroma (pasta should be color of peanut butter), 6 to 10 minutes. Move pasta to a container. Wipe out frying pan using paper towels.

4. Heat remaining 2 tablespoons oil in now-empty frying pan on moderate to high heat until it starts to shimmer. Put in onion and ¼ teaspoon salt and cook till they become tender and starting to brown around edges, four to eight minutes. Put in tomatoes and cook, stirring intermittently, until mixture is thick, dry, and slightly darkened in color, four to eight minutes. Decrease heat to medium, put in remaining garlic, paprika, smoked paprika, and anchovy paste, and cook until aromatic, about 1½ minutes. Mix in pasta until combined. Place oven rack 5 to 6 inches from broiler element and heat broiler.

5. Pour shrimp broth through fine-mesh strainer into skillet; discard shells. Put in wine, ¼ teaspoon salt, and ½ teaspoon pepper and stir well. Increase heat to medium-high and bring to simmer. Cook, stirring intermittently, until liquid is slightly thickened and pasta is just tender, eight to ten minutes. Scatter shrimp over pasta and stir to partially submerge. Move frying pan to oven and broil until shrimp are opaque and surface of pasta is dry with crisped, browned spots, 5 to 7 minutes. Remove from oven and let sit, uncovered, for about five minutes. Sprinkle with parsley and serve instantly with lemon wedges.

Spicy Beefy Rigatoni

Yield: 6 Servings

Ingredients:

- ½ cup dry red wine
- ½ teaspoon ground cinnamon
- 1 (28-ounce) can whole peeled tomatoes, drained with juice reserved, chopped fine
- 1 onion, chopped fine
- 1 pound rigatoni
- 1 tablespoon extra-virgin olive oil
- 1 teaspoon minced fresh thyme or ¼ teaspoon dried
- 1½ pounds bone-in English-style short ribs, trimmed

- 2 tablespoons minced fresh parsley
- 3 garlic cloves, minced
- Grated Parmesan cheese
- Pinch ground cloves
- Salt and pepper

Directions:

1. Pat ribs dry using paper towels and sprinkle with salt and pepper. Heat oil in 12-inch frying pan on moderate to high heat until just smoking. Brown ribs on all sides, eight to ten minutes; move to plate.
2. Pour off all but 1 teaspoon fat from skillet, put in onion, and cook on moderate heat till they become tender, approximately five minutes. Mix in garlic, thyme, cinnamon, and cloves and cook until aromatic, approximately half a minute. Mix in wine, scraping up any browned bits, and simmer until nearly evaporated, approximately two minutes.
3. Mix in tomatoes and reserved juice. Nestle ribs into sauce along with any accumulated juices and bring to simmer. Decrease heat to low, cover, and simmer gently, turning ribs occasionally, until meat is very soft and falling off bones, about 2 hours.
4. Move ribs to slicing board, allow to cool slightly, then shred meat into bite-size pieces using 2 forks; discard excess fat and bones. Using wide, shallow spoon, skim excess fat from surface of sauce. Stir shredded meat and any accumulated juices into sauce and bring to simmer on moderate heat. Sprinkle with salt and pepper to taste.
5. In the meantime, bring 4 quarts water to boil in large pot. Put in pasta and 1 tablespoon salt and cook, stirring frequently, until al dente. Reserve ½ cup cooking water, then drain pasta and return it to pot. Put in sauce and parsley and toss to combine. Sprinkle with salt and pepper to taste and regulate consistency with reserved cooking water as required. Serve with Parmesan.

Tangy Penne with Fresh Tomato Sauce

Yield: 6 Servings

�./ This recipe can be made quickly �./

Ⓥ This is a Vegetarian Recipe Ⓥ

Ingredients:

- ⅛ teaspoon red pepper flakes
- ¼ cup extra-virgin olive oil
- ½ teaspoon fennel seeds, crushed
- 1 fennel bulb, stalks discarded, bulb halved, cored, and cut into ¼-inch pieces
- 1 pound penne
- 2 (3-inch) strips orange zest plus 3 tablespoons juice
- 2 garlic cloves, minced
- 3 pounds ripe tomatoes, cored, peeled, seeded, and cut into ½-inch pieces
- 3 tablespoons chopped fresh basil
- Pinch saffron threads, crumbled (optional)
- Salt and pepper
- Sugar

Directions:

1. Heat 2 tablespoons oil in 12-inch frying pan on moderate heat until it starts to shimmer. Put in fennel and cook till they become tender and lightly browned, 5 to 7 minutes. Mix in garlic, orange zest, fennel seeds, pepper flakes, and saffron, if using, and cook until aromatic, approximately half a minute. Mix in tomatoes and cook until tomato pieces lose their shape and make chunky sauce, about 10 minutes. Discard orange zest.
2. In the meantime, bring 4 quarts water to boil in large pot. Put in pasta and 1 tablespoon salt and cook, stirring frequently, until al dente. Reserve ½ cup cooking water, then drain pasta and return it to pot.

3. Stir orange juice, basil, ¼ teaspoon salt, and ⅛ teaspoon pepper into sauce and season with sugar to taste. Put in sauce and remaining 2 tablespoons oil to pasta and toss to combine. Sprinkle with salt and pepper to taste and regulate consistency with reserved cooking water as required. Serve.

Whole-Wheat Spaghetti Mix

Yield: 6 Servings

Ⓥ *This is a Vegetarian Recipe* Ⓥ

Ingredients:

- ¼–½ teaspoon red pepper flakes
- ¾ cup pitted kalamata olives, chopped coarse
- ¾ cup vegetable broth
- 1 (14.5-ounce) can diced tomatoes, drained
- 1 (15-ounce) can cannellini beans, rinsed
- 1 onion, chopped fine
- 1 pound whole-wheat spaghetti
- 1¼ pounds curly-leaf spinach, stemmed and cut into 1-inch pieces
- 2 ounces Parmesan cheese, grated (1 cup), plus extra for serving
- 3 tablespoons extra-virgin olive oil, plus extra for serving
- 8 garlic cloves, peeled (5 sliced thin along the length, 3 minced)
- Salt and pepper

Directions:

1. Cook oil and sliced garlic in 12-inch straight-sided sauté pan on moderate heat, stirring frequently, until garlic turns golden but not brown, approximately three minutes. Use a slotted spoon to move garlic to plate coated using paper towels and season lightly with salt; set aside.
2. Put in onion to oil left in pan and cook on moderate heat till they become tender and lightly browned, 5 to 7 minutes. Mix in

minced garlic and pepper flakes and cook until aromatic, approximately half a minute. Put in half of spinach and cook, tossing occasionally, until starting to wilt, approximately two minutes. Put in remaining spinach, broth, tomatoes, and ¾ teaspoon salt and bring to simmer. Decrease heat to medium, cover (pan will be very full), and cook, tossing occasionally, until spinach is completely wilted, about 10 minutes (mixture will be somewhat soupy). Remove from the heat, mix in beans and olives.

3. In the meantime, bring 4 quarts water to boil in large pot. Put in pasta and 1 tablespoon salt and cook, stirring frequently, until just shy of al dente. Reserve ½ cup cooking water, then drain pasta and return it to pot. Put in greens mixture and cook on moderate heat, tossing to combine, until pasta absorbs most of liquid, approximately two minutes.

4. Remove from the heat, mix in Parmesan. Sprinkle with salt and pepper to taste and regulate consistency with reserved cooking water as required. Serve, sprinkling individual portions with garlic chips and extra Parmesan and drizzling with extra oil.

Zucchini-Tomatoes Farfalle

Yield: **6 Servings**

Ⓥ This is a Vegetarian Recipe Ⓥ

Ingredients:

- ¼ cup chopped fresh mint
- ½ cup pitted kalamata olives, quartered
- 1 pound farfalle
- 1 red onion, chopped fine
- 1 teaspoon grated lemon zest plus 1 tablespoon juice
- 12 ounces grape tomatoes, halved
- 2 pounds zucchini and/or summer squash, halved along the length and sliced ½ inch thick

- 2 teaspoons red wine vinegar
- 3 garlic cloves, minced
- 4 ounces feta cheese, crumbled (1 cup)
- 5 tablespoons extra-virgin olive oil
- Kosher salt and pepper

Directions:

1. Toss squash with 1 tablespoon salt and allow to drain using a colander for 30 minutes. Pat squash dry using paper towels and carefully wipe away any residual salt.
2. Heat 1 tablespoon oil in 12-inch non-stick frying pan on high heat until just smoking. Put in half of squash and cook, stirring intermittently, until golden brown and smildly charred, 5 to 7 minutes, reducing heat if frying pan begins to scorch; move to large plate. Repeat with 1 tablespoon oil and remaining squash; move to plate.
3. Heat 1 tablespoon oil in now-empty frying pan on moderate heat until it starts to shimmer. Put in onion and cook till they become tender and lightly browned, 5 to 7 minutes. Mix in garlic, lemon zest, and ½ teaspoon pepper and cook until aromatic, approximately half a minute. Mix in squash and cook until heated through, approximately half a minute.
4. In the meantime, bring 4 quarts water to boil in large pot. Put in pasta and 1 tablespoon salt and cook, stirring frequently, until al dente. Reserve ½ cup cooking water, then drain pasta and return it to pot. Put in squash mixture, tomatoes, olives, mint, vinegar, lemon juice, and remaining 2 tablespoons oil and toss to combine. Sprinkle with salt and pepper to taste and regulate consistency with reserved cooking water as required. Serve, passing feta seperately.

Couscous

Couscous is a staple food throughout the North African cuisines of Morocco, Algeria, Tunisia, Mauritania, and Libya.

Basic Couscous

Yield: 6 Servings

�254 This recipe can be made quickly �254

Ⓥ This is a Vegetarian Recipe Ⓥ

Ingredients:

- 1 cup chicken or vegetable broth
- 1 cup water
- 2 cups couscous
- 2 tablespoons extra-virgin olive oil
- Salt and pepper

Directions:

1. Heat oil in moderate-sized saucepan on moderate to high heat until it starts to shimmer. Put in couscous and cook, stirring often, until grains are just starting to brown, 3 to 5 minutes.
2. Mix in water, broth, and 1 teaspoon salt. Cover, remove saucepan from heat, and allow to sit until couscous is tender, approximately seven minutes. Gently fluff couscous with fork and season with pepper to taste. Serve.

Basic Couscous with Carrots, Raisins, and Pine Nuts

�254 This recipe can be made quickly �254

Ⓥ This is a Vegetarian Recipe Ⓥ

Increase oil to 3 tablespoons. Before adding couscous to saucepan, put in 2 peeled and grated carrots and ½ teaspoon ground cinnamon and cook till they become tender, approximately two minutes. Put in ½ cup raisins to saucepan with couscous and increase water to 1¼ cups. Before you serve, mix in ⅓ cup toasted pine nuts, 3 tablespoons minced fresh cilantro, ½ teaspoon grated orange zest, and 1 tablespoon orange juice.

Basic Couscous with Dates and Pistachios

This recipe can be made quickly

Ⓥ This is a Vegetarian Recipe Ⓥ

Increase oil to 3 tablespoons. Put in ½ cup chopped pitted dates, 1 tablespoon grated fresh ginger, and ½ teaspoon ground cardamom to saucepan with couscous. Increase water to 1¼ cups. Before you serve, mix in ¾ cup coarsely chopped toasted pistachios, 3 tablespoons minced fresh cilantro, and 2 teaspoons lemon juice.

Basic Pearl Couscous

Yield: 6 Servings

This recipe can be made quickly

Ⓥ This is a Vegetarian Recipe Ⓥ

Ingredients:

- ½ teaspoon salt
- 1 tablespoon extra-virgin olive oil
- 2 cups pearl couscous
- 2½ cups water

Directions:

1. Heat couscous and oil in moderate-sized saucepan on moderate heat, stirring often, until about half of grains start to look golden brown, approximately five minutes.
2. Mix in water and salt, increase heat to high, and bring to boil. Decrease heat to moderate to low, cover, and simmer, stirring intermittently, until water is absorbed and couscous is tender, 9 to 12 minutes. Remove from the heat, let couscous sit, covered, for about three minutes. Serve.

Basic Pearl Couscous Wholesome Mix

Yield: 6 Servings

Ⓥ This is a Vegetarian Recipe Ⓥ

Ingredients:

- ¼ teaspoon ground cardamom
- 1 (15-ounce) can great Northern beans, rinsed
- 1 onion, chopped
- 1 pound eggplant, cut into ½-inch pieces
- 1 tablespoon tomato paste
- 1 teaspoon ground fenugreek
- 1 teaspoon ground sumac
- 1½ cups pearl couscous
- 2 cups chicken or vegetable broth
- 3 garlic cloves, minced
- 3 ounces (3 cups) baby spinach
- 5 tablespoons extra-virgin olive oil, plus extra for serving
- Salt and pepper

Directions:

1. Mix sumac, fenugreek, ½ teaspoon salt, ½ teaspoon pepper, and cardamom in a small-sized container. Line large plate using double layer of coffee filters and spray using vegetable oil spray. Toss eggplant with ½ teaspoon spice mixture and spread

uniformly coffee filters. Microwave eggplant, uncovered, until dry to touch and slightly shriveled, 7 to 10 minutes, tossing halfway through microwaving.

2. Heat couscous and 2 tablespoons oil in 12-inch non-stick frying pan on moderate heat, stirring often, until about half of grains start to look golden brown, approximately five minutes. Move to a container and wipe frying pan clean using paper towels.

3. Toss eggplant with 1 teaspoon spice mixture. Heat 1 tablespoon oil in now-empty frying pan on moderate to high heat until it starts to shimmer. Put in eggplant and cook, stirring intermittently, until well browned, 5 to 7 minutes. Move to different container.

4. Heat remaining 2 tablespoons oil in again-empty frying pan on moderate heat until it starts to shimmer. Put in onion and cook till they become tender and lightly browned, 5 to 7 minutes. Mix in garlic, tomato paste, and remaining spice mixture and cook until aromatic, about 1 minute.

5. Mix in broth, beans, and couscous and bring to simmer. Decrease heat to moderate to low, cover, and simmer, stirring intermittently, until broth is absorbed and couscous is tender, 9 to 12 minutes. Remove from the heat, mix in spinach and eggplant, cover, and allow to sit for about three minutes. Sprinkle with salt and pepper to taste and drizzle with extra oil. Serve.

Basic Pearl Couscous with Peas, Feta, and Pickled Shallots

Yield: 6 Servings

Ⓥ This is a Vegetarian Recipe Ⓥ

Ingredients:

- ⅛ teaspoon red pepper flakes
- ¼ cup extra-virgin olive oil
- ⅓ cup red wine vinegar

- ½ cup frozen peas, thawed
- ½ cup shelled pistachios, toasted and chopped
- 1 cup fresh mint leaves, torn
- 1 teaspoon Dijon mustard
- 2 cups pearl couscous
- 2 shallots, sliced thin
- 2 tablespoons sugar
- 2½ cups water
- 3 ounces feta cheese, crumbled (¾ cup)
- 3 tablespoons lemon juice
- 4 ounces (4 cups) baby arugula, coarsely chopped
- Salt and pepper

Directions:

1. Heat 1 tablespoon oil and couscous in moderate-sized saucepan on moderate heat, stirring often, until about half of grains start to look golden brown, approximately five minutes. Mix in water and ½ teaspoon salt, increase heat to high, and bring to boil. Decrease heat to moderate to low, cover, and simmer, stirring intermittently, until water is absorbed and couscous is tender, 9 to 12 minutes. Remove from the heat, let couscous sit, covered, for about three minutes. Move couscous to rimmed baking sheet and allow to cool completely, about fifteen minutes.

2. In the meantime, bring vinegar, sugar, and pinch salt to simmer in small saucepan on moderate to high heat, stirring intermittently, until sugar dissolves. Put in shallots and stir to combine. Remove from heat, cover, and allow to cool completely, approximately half an hour. Drain and discard liquid.

3. Beat remaining 3 tablespoons oil, lemon juice, mustard, pepper flakes, and ⅛ teaspoon salt together in a big container. Put in couscous, arugula, mint, peas, 6 tablespoons pistachios, ½ cup feta, and shallots and gently toss to combine. Sprinkle with salt and pepper to taste and move to serving bowl. Allow to sit for about five minutes. Sprinkle with remaining ¼ cup feta and remaining 2 tablespoons pistachios and serve.

Basic Pearl Couscous with Radishes and Watercress

Yield: 6 Servings

Ⓥ *This is a Vegetarian Recipe* Ⓥ

Ingredients:

- ¼ cup extra-virgin olive oil
- ¼ teaspoon sugar
- ½ cup walnuts, toasted and chopped coarse
- 1 teaspoon Dijon mustard
- 1 teaspoon smoked paprika
- 1½ cups coarsely chopped parsley
- 2 cups pearl couscous
- 2 ounces (2 cups) watercress, torn into bite-size pieces
- 2½ cups water
- 3 tablespoons sherry vinegar
- 4 ounces goat cheese, crumbled (1 cup)
- 6 radishes, trimmed and cut into matchsticks
- 6 scallions, sliced thin
- Salt and pepper

Directions:

1. Heat 1 tablespoon oil and couscous in moderate-sized saucepan on moderate heat, stirring often, until about half of grains start to look golden brown, approximately five minutes. Mix in water and ½ teaspoon salt, increase heat to high, and bring to boil. Decrease heat to moderate to low, cover, and simmer, stirring intermittently, until water is absorbed and couscous is tender, 9 to 12 minutes. Remove from the heat, let couscous sit, covered, for about three minutes. Move couscous to rimmed baking sheet and allow to cool completely, about fifteen minutes.
2. Beat vinegar, mustard, paprika, sugar, ⅛ teaspoon salt, and remaining 3 tablespoons oil together in a big container. Put in

couscous, watercress, scallions, radishes, parsley, and 6 tablespoons walnuts and gently toss to combine. Sprinkle with salt and pepper to taste and move to serving bowl. Allow to sit for about five minutes. Sprinkle with goat cheese and remaining 2 tablespoons walnuts and serve.

Basic Pearl Couscous with Tomatoes, Olives, and Ricotta Salata

Yield: 6 Servings

Ⓥ *This is a Vegetarian Recipe* Ⓥ

Ingredients:

- ¼ cup extra-virgin olive oil
- ¼ cup minced fresh chives
- ½ cup pine nuts, toasted
- ⅔ cup pitted kalamata olives, sliced
- 1 teaspoon Dijon mustard
- 1½ cups coarsely chopped fresh basil
- 12 ounces grape tomatoes, quartered
- 2 cups pearl couscous
- 2 ounces (2 cups) baby spinach, sliced ¼ inch thick
- 2½ cups water
- 3 ounces ricotta salata cheese, crumbled (¾ cup)
- 3 tablespoons red wine vinegar
- Salt and pepper

Directions:

1. Heat 1 tablespoon oil and couscous in moderate-sized saucepan on moderate heat, stirring often, until about half of grains start to look golden brown, approximately five minutes. Mix in water and ½ teaspoon salt, increase heat to high, and bring to boil. Decrease heat to moderate to low, cover, and simmer, stirring

intermittently, until water is absorbed and couscous is tender, 9 to 12 minutes. Remove from the heat, let couscous sit, covered, for about three minutes. Move couscous to rimmed baking sheet and allow to cool completely, about fifteen minutes.

2. Beat vinegar, mustard, ⅛ teaspoon salt, and remaining 3 tablespoons oil together in a big container. Put in couscous, tomatoes, spinach, basil, ½ cup ricotta salata, olives, 6 tablespoons pine nuts, and chives and gently toss to combine. Sprinkle with salt and pepper to taste and move to serving bowl. Allow to sit for about five minutes. Sprinkle with remaining ¼ cup ricotta salata and remaining 2 tablespoons pine nuts and serve.

Lemony Sujuk Couscous

Yield: 6 Servings

This recipe can be made quickly

Feel free to substitute Sujuk with any other dry-cured meat if you cannot find it.

Ingredients:

- ¼ cup chopped fresh cilantro
- ¼ preserved lemon, pulp and white pith removed, rind rinsed and minced (1 tablespoon)
- ¼ teaspoon ground cardamom
- ½ cup golden raisins
- 1 onion, chopped fine
- 1½ cups couscous
- 1¾ cups vegetable broth
- 2 carrots, peeled and chopped fine
- 3 garlic cloves, minced
- 3 tablespoons extra-virgin olive oil
- 4 ounces sujuk (Turkish dry-cured beef sausage) sausage, chopped fine
- Salt and pepper

Directions:

1. Heat 2 tablespoons oil in 12-inch frying pan on moderate to high heat until it starts to shimmer. Put in couscous and cook, stirring often, until grains are just starting to brown, 3 to 5 minutes. Move to a container and wipe frying pan clean using paper towels.
2. Heat residual 1 tablespoon oil in now-empty frying pan on moderate heat until it starts to shimmer. Put in sujuk, onion, carrots, ¼ teaspoon salt, and ¼ teaspoon pepper and cook until vegetables are softened and lightly browned, six to eight minutes. Mix in preserved lemon, garlic, and cardamom and cook until aromatic, approximately half a minute. Mix in broth and bring to simmer.
3. Mix in raisins and couscous. Cover, remove frying pan from heat, and allow to sit until couscous is tender, approximately seven minutes. Put in cilantro to couscous and gently fluff with fork to combine. Sprinkle with salt and pepper to taste. Serve.

Moroccan Chickpea Couscous

Yield: 6 Servings

⚡ This recipe can be made quickly ⚡

Ⓥ This is a Vegetarian Recipe Ⓥ

Ingredients:

- ¼ cup extra-virgin olive oil, plus extra for serving
- ¼ teaspoon ground anise seed
- ½ cup chopped fresh parsley, cilantro, and/or mint
- 1 (15-ounce) can chickpeas, rinsed
- 1 onion, chopped fine
- 1 teaspoon ground coriander
- 1 teaspoon ground ginger
- 1½ cups couscous

- 1½ cups frozen peas
- 1¾ cups chicken or vegetable broth
- 2 carrots, peeled and chopped fine
- 3 garlic cloves, minced
- Lemon wedges
- Salt and pepper

Directions:

1. Heat 2 tablespoons oil in 12-inch frying pan on moderate to high heat until it starts to shimmer. Put in couscous and cook, stirring often, until grains are just starting to brown, 3 to 5 minutes. Move to a container and wipe frying pan clean using paper towels.
2. Heat remaining 2 tablespoons oil in now-empty frying pan on moderate heat until it starts to shimmer. Put in carrots, onion, and 1 teaspoon salt and cook till they become tender and lightly browned, 5 to 7 minutes. Mix in garlic, coriander, ginger, and anise and cook until aromatic, approximately half a minute. Mix in broth and chickpeas and bring to simmer.
3. Mix in peas and couscous. Cover, remove frying pan from heat, and allow to sit until couscous is tender, approximately seven minutes. Put in parsley to couscous and gently fluff with fork to combine. Sprinkle with salt and pepper to taste and drizzle with extra oil. Serve with lemon wedges.

Spicy Vegge Couscous

Yield: 6 Servings

Ⓥ This is a Vegetarian Recipe Ⓥ

Ingredients:

- 1 head cauliflower (2 pounds), cored and cut into 1-inch florets
- 1 red bell pepper, stemmed, seeded, and cut into ½-inch pieces
- 1 tablespoon minced fresh marjoram

- 1 teaspoon grated lemon zest, plus lemon wedges for serving
- 1 zucchini, cut into ½-inch pieces
- 1½ cups couscous
- 1¾ cups chicken or vegetable broth
- 2 teaspoons ras el hanout
- 4 garlic cloves, minced
- 6 tablespoons extra-virgin olive oil, plus extra for serving
- Salt and pepper

Directions:

1. Toss cauliflower with 2 tablespoons oil, ¾ teaspoon salt, and ½ teaspoon pepper in 12-inch non-stick skillet. Cover and cook on moderate to high heat until florets start to brown and edges just start to become translucent (do not lift lid), approximately five minutes.
2. Remove lid and continue to cook, stirring every 2 minutes, until florets turn golden brown in several spots, about 10 minutes. Move to a container and wipe frying pan clean using paper towels.
3. Heat 2 tablespoons oil in now-empty frying pan on moderate to high heat until it starts to shimmer. Put in couscous and cook, stirring often, until grains are just starting to brown, 3 to 5 minutes. Move to different container and wipe frying pan clean using paper towels.
4. Heat remaining 2 tablespoons oil in again-empty frying pan on moderate to high heat until just smoking. Put in zucchini, bell pepper, and ½ teaspoon salt and cook until tender, six to eight minutes. Mix in garlic, ras el hanout, and lemon zest and cook until aromatic, approximately half a minute. Mix in broth and bring to simmer.
5. Mix in couscous. Cover, remove frying pan from heat, and allow to sit until couscous is tender, approximately seven minutes. Put in cauliflower and marjoram to couscous and gently fluff with fork to combine. Sprinkle with salt and pepper to taste and drizzle with extra oil. Serve with lemon wedges.

Tangy Lamb-Chickpea Couscous

Yield: 6 Servings

Ingredients:

- ⅛ teaspoon cayenne pepper
- ¼ teaspoon ground cinnamon
- ⅓ cup minced fresh parsley
- ½ cup dry white wine
- ½ cup raisins
- ½ cup sliced almonds, toasted
- 1 (15-ounce) can chickpeas, rinsed
- 1 onion, chopped fine
- 1 pound lamb shoulder chops (blade or round bone), 1 to 1½ inches thick, trimmed and halved
- 1 teaspoon grated fresh ginger
- 1 teaspoon ground coriander
- 10 (2-inch) strips orange zest (1 orange)
- 1½ cups couscous
- 2½ cups chicken broth
- 3 tablespoons extra-virgin olive oil, plus extra for serving
- Salt and pepper

Directions:

1. Place oven rack to lower-middle position and pre-heat your oven to 325 degrees. Heat 2 tablespoons oil in a Dutch oven on moderate to high heat until it starts to shimmer. Put in couscous and cook, stirring often, until grains are just starting to brown, 3 to 5 minutes. Move to a container and wipe pot clean using paper towels.
2. Pat lamb dry using paper towels and sprinkle with salt and pepper. Heat residual 1 tablespoon oil in now-empty pot on moderate to high heat until just smoking. Brown lamb, about 4 minutes each side; move to plate.
3. Put in onion to fat left in pot and cook on moderate heat till they become tender, approximately five minutes. Mix in orange zest,

ginger, coriander, cinnamon, cayenne, and ⅛ teaspoon pepper and cook until aromatic, approximately half a minute. Mix in wine, scraping up any browned bits. Mix in broth and chickpeas and bring to boil.

4. Nestle lamb into pot along with any accumulated juices. Cover, place pot in oven, and cook until fork slips easily in and out of lamb, about 1 hour.

5. Move lamb to slicing board, allow to cool slightly, then shred into bite-size pieces using 2 forks, discarding excess fat and bones. Strain cooking liquid through fine mesh strainer set over bowl. Return solids and 1½ cups cooking liquid to now-empty pot and bring to simmer on moderate heat; discard remaining liquid.

6. Mix in couscous and raisins. Cover, remove pot from heat, and allow to sit until couscous is tender, approximately seven minutes. Put in shredded lamb, almonds, and parsley to couscous and gently fluff with fork to combine. Sprinkle with salt and pepper to taste and drizzle with extra oil. Serve.

Endnote

Thank you for purchasing this book. If you enjoyed this book, check out other Mediterranean Diet cookbooks by Nadine Massri. Also, don't forget to leave a review on amazon!